W9-BFQ-147

Small Reef Aquarium Basics

The Optimum Aquarium for the Reef Hobbyist

Albert J. Thiel

Author of
The Marine Fish and Invert Reef Aquarium
Advanced Reef Keeping Made Simple (I)

Aardvark Press
575 Broad Street
Bridgeport, CT 06604

Distributed exclusively by :

Energy Savers Unlimited
Torrance, California
1-800 678 8844

Published by :
Aardvark Press
575 Broad Street
Bridgeport, CT 06604

Fon (203) 368 2111
Fax (203) 367 5872

The Optimum Aquarium for the Reef Hobbyist

Set in Souvenir Laser Typeface from Adobe
using Pagemaker 3.0 from Aldus
on a Dynamac Computer with E-Machines' large display Monitor

Others Books by Albert J. Thiel :

• The Marine Fish and Invert Reef Aquarium
• Advanced Reef Keeping Made Simple
• Marine Reef, the Newsletter on Reef Tanks

Exclusive Distributors :
Energy Savers Unlimited
Torrance, California
1-800-678 8844

ISBN - 0945777 02 7

Small Reef Aquarium Basics

is dedicated to all Hobbyists who would

like to enter the Reef Keeping Hobby

but maintain smaller aquariums

and do not necessarily want to equip

their tank with Hi-Tech instruments

and products.

"It all boils down to water chemistry"

Introduction

The interest in Reef Aquariums has recently grown in popularity so rapidly, that everyone, including Pet Store Owners and personnel, have a hard time keeping up with all the developments that are occuring. New filtration methods, and new equipment, appear in the magazines, and in advertising, every month.

Newer methods for keeping such aquariums, including very hi-tech instrumentation, are being advocated all the time. Sophisticated testing is recommended as well. In short, a completely different approach than the one Hobbyists and Stores have been accustomed to, leading to a lot of confusing and misunderstandings, especially since some of the recommendations have not been tested over long periods of time yet, and may even conflict.

Although books such as "The Marine Fish and Invert Reef Aquarium", and "Advanced Reef Keeping Made Simple" have obviously helped a great deal, both are concerned with larger systems. Tanks in the 100 to 150 gallon range, a size that not many Hobbyists keep and that requires more sophistication, and the related expenses, because of the greater amount of animal life that is kept in such aquariums.

Of course, the methods advocated there, can be applied to smaller aquariums as well, but increase the budget required to get into Reef Keeping quite a bit.

Many Store Owners, and many Hobbyists, have suggested that I write a book geared more specifically to the Reef Keeper who wishes to maintain a small system successfully without having to spend thousands of dollars. Very instrumental in convincing me to undertake this project was **Roger Paro, of Kenlin Pet Supplies**, in Mahwah, New Jersey. This manuscript is, therefore, the product of all the suggestions received, and a little arm twisting from some.

The book is shorter than my other ones, mainly because interested readers can refer to both of them for a more detailed look at some of the subjects covered here. Additionally some of the equipment discussed in the other books is not used in the set up that I would like to suggest for the smaller aquarium.

The real basics of aquarium keeping are not covered in this book. You should refer to one of the many other books available for more details on, e.g. heating; biological filtration, and why and how it takes place; stands; tanks; fish, other animals, background information, etc...

One such book that is strongly recommended is Martin A. Moe Jr.'s " **The Marine Aquarium Reference - Systems and Invertebrates**" 1989, 510 pp, Green Turtle Publications. It contains a wealth of information and techniques that you may want to consider when setting up your new Reef Tank, or when making modifications to an existing aquarium. It is brand new and incorporates very up-to-date information, drawing on the latest technology available, and very recent texts, articles and books.

Martin Moe's contributions to the Hobby already stood out with his first book, "**Marine Aquarium Handbook, Beginner to Breeder**" this one tops it. Every serious Hobbyist should get a copy of it. It is available from stores nationwide.

Do not overlook the many books published by **T.F.H. Publications** either, they are, after all, the largest publishers of Aquarium literature in the world, and have books on many subjects of interest to the Reef Keeping Hobbyist. Your local Pet Store will usually have a wide assortment of their books.

What we are trying to achieve in this one, is setting up a Reef Tank on a budget! You may still have to spend more money than what you would lay out for a regular fish tank, but it certainly will not be a budget that resembles anything like the tanks described in both my other books, where most functions are automated; or where I describe how you can introduce such automation, and what your options are.

No tank can be set up for two or three hundred dollars, but by following the directions in this guide you should be able to considerably reduce the cost of what you thought installing such a tank would necessitate. The cost of the aquarium and the stand are not part of what we will be reviewing. You may have both already, or you may want to shop around for a special. Pet Stores have them all the time. Alternatively look in your local bargain newspaper. Fish tanks are advertised in such newspapers every week, and at excellent prices. You may even find some of the equipment you will need as well.

Because Reef Keeping is complex, much more so than just plain fish-only tanks, the selection of the items that you will be using is important. Buy products that will last you for a long time. Avoid the "store-them-in-the-garage-or-attic and replace-them-with-something-else syndrome" so characteristic of what a lot of us have been doing in the past.

By buying the right product, of the right quality, you will buy only once. Let me illustrate this, for example, if you need an overflow surface-skimming syphon, and 3 are offered for sale, don't buy the cheapest one. Unless of course that happens to be the one that you need for your tank.

First determine what you need, then select what to buy. If you are looking at running several hundred gallons of water per hour, a syphon with half inch connections will not do the job, even though it may be the cheapest. All that will happen is that after a few weeks you will get tired of messing around with it, having determined that it does'nt really do the job, and end up buying a more expensive one anyway. As a result you end up spending more money than if you had bought the right one to begin with.

Determining what your exact needs are is half the battle. Once you know what you need, you can start looking around for the product that meets the specifications you have found to be necessary. That product will not become obsolete in a couple of weeks or months, because it will be the right one for the job.

Another example is the redox potential meter. A meter alone will only tell you what the redox is. Soon you may get the urge to control it. A meter cannot do that. You will then want, and need, a redox potential controller. This is a different piece of equipment, that you will then need to buy, and it will obsolete the meter. The money spent on the meter will have been wasted. Think before buying and decide what it really is that you will want to do. Of course, in a small system you may not want to automate, and then a meter will do fine.

Ask questions about the equipment. For instance, in the case of controllers, either for pH or redox potential, many less expensive models are so-called "panel mount" types, requiring hard wiring and having no full external cover.

What you are probably looking for is a so-called "bench top" model, one in which you can just plug in the device (e.g. ozone, chemical metering pump, peristaltic pump) that you are trying to control, without any wiring whatsoever.

Keep these remarks in mind every time you need to acquire some piece of equipment or instrument. They will save you a lot of money in the long run.

Reef Keeping is fascinating and it can be great fun, but you must meet certain minimum requirements in water quality, or your tank just will not look good. What these parameters are, and how to attain them on a smaller budget is the purpose of this book.

Setting up a Reef Tank will still cost a fair amount of money, but using the methods described here, a lot less than if you went with a full-fledged automated system such as the ones described in my other two books, or often referred to in Marine Reef, the newsletter of which I have the pleasure of being the Editor. Such systems are of course much more self-sufficient, but obviously at a cost.

We hope that the recommendations made in this book will help, and welcome suggestions for inclusion in future editions, and reprints. If we have overlooked something, if a particular method has worked for you, let us know about it.

Sharing knowledge is what it's all about.

As a final note, don't expect any miracles, successful aquarium keeping is a combination of a fair amount of knowledge, common sense practices, and the right equipment. Good luck in your endeavors.

Albert J. Thiel
Trumbull, Connecticut

A special note of thanks to Guido Hueckstedt,
whose contributions to the Hobby, and
research, are so often overlooked.

We also wish to acknowledge :

Martin A. Moe

and most of all

Sarah R. Thiel
for her patience and understanding
during the writing of this manuscript.
Her support was invaluable to me.

Filtration

■ General Remarks

All, or almost all, successful Reef Systems that I have ever seen have one thing in common: **they segregate the various modes of filtration required to maintain optimum water quality levels and chemistry.** We should try to learn from that empyric evidence, and duplicate the methods used by such successful Reef Keeping Hobbyists.

The various segregated methods of filtration that I am referring to here, include the following, most of which you are familiar with to some extent:

• Mechanical filtration, or fine and micron:sub-micron filtration, to remove so-called detritus or particulate matter from the water
• Biological filtration, to break down ammonia, nitrite, and convert the latter to nitrate,
• Chemical filtration to remove pollutants that the 2 methods mentioned above do not,
• Foam fractionation, to remove e.g. protein before it breaks down further and pollutes the water,
• Pressure filters - contact chambers for oxygen and ozone, this includes, for example, oxygen reactors, ozone reactors and such,
• Miscellaneous methods, e.g. denitrators, specialized resins, tangential flow filters, biomesh filters, Aerobic nitrate filters, etc.

Some of these will, for obvious reasons, not be used on the small Reef System that we are dealing with in this book: they are meant to be used on more automated systems, and several of them involve quite a considerable expense. Pressurized contact chambers such as oxygen reactors, for instance, can cost around $ 250.00, and tangential flow filters quite a bit more.

Filtration is of course the one important aspect of the total system that determines whether your Reef will be successful or not. It is, indeed, through proper filtration that the water is cleansed of impurities and unwanted compounds and chemicals. This, then, ensures a proper living environment for the fish and invertebrates kept in the tank. Because you add fish, corals and invertebrates, the water quality deteriorates; there is no way around it. A real minimum amount of filtration, that you cannot do without, is, as a result, necessary for you to be a successful reef Hobbyist, as it will remove those unwanted noxious elements.

Everything ultimately boils down to the quality of the water. The better that quality, the better your Reef Aquarium will look. The worse the water chemistry, the worse the tank will look, and the more life forms will die, which in turn leads to even more problems. **Polluted water is the nemesis of every Aquarist.**

The accumulation of breakdown products of organic and non-organic nature will eventually drop the quality of the water so much, that the tank turns into an environment not suitable for animals. Keep it in mind ! And if you do not take care of your system this can happen in a matter of days, sometimes even hours. Fish and invertebrates take the abuse for a while, and then suddenly things will deteriorate very quickly, often to the Hobbyist's surprise, as only a few hours earlier everything "seemed" to be fine.

Good water chemistry does not happen by chance, it can be attained only in 2 major ways: continuous water changes (the so-called completely open system), or proper and well maintained filtration of at least four kinds, the ones listed higher up, mechanical, biological, chemical and foam fractionation. Fortunately for us, three of these four can nowadays be combined in one unit: **the trickle filter**. Not all trickle filters on the market, however, offer this feature. If you are in the market for one, check whether the filter that you are looking to acquire incorporates the required filtration steps on one hand, and does so in a segregated fashion on the other, allowing you to control and service mechanical, biological and chemical filtration separately, and in their own right without affecting anything else.

Only when such is possible, will you be able to work on your filters to service and maintain them, without affecting what is happening to the others. Mechanical filters need very regular cleaning, chemical filters need to be changed from time to time and rinsed to remove detritus, **whereas biological filters should always be left alone**.

Bacteria in the biological filters (chamber) should not be disturbed by the cleaning process, or by moving the material on which they grow, around or in and out of the filters. Doing so always results in a loss of bacteria, and a considerable reduction in the efficiency of the filters. The latter may result in an increase in ammonia and nitrite and stress to tank life forms. Stress often brings about disease. Usually parasitic disease. The latter is very hard to treat in Reef Tanks, as no copper or similar compounds can be used, because of the invertebrates in the tank. Both stress and disease can rapidly lead to massive outbreaks of parasitic infestations because one infected fish, acting as a host, brings about a rapid multiplication of parasites, which then attack other fish. A real vicious circle which is then very hard to control.

Filtration, and how its various components are set up is, therefore, very important for the long time appearance and health of the aquarium. The selection of the components of the filtration system must, as a result, be carefully planned and thought out in advance.

Many Hobbyists pay little or no attention to mechanical filtration. That is a considerable mistake. Mechanical filtration is, indeed, an important part of maintaining adequate water chemistry parameters. Biological filtration does get a lot of attention, perhaps too much somtimes. Chemical filtration is going through a growth stage, and more and more Hobbyists are starting to realize its importance, which is an excellent trend, of course.

In the subsequent chapters we will take a more in depth look at each of these strongly recommended forms of water filtration, and suggest how they should be incorportated in a small reef aquarium.

■ Mechanical Filtration

Mechanical filtration is nothing more than removing many types of unwanted particulate matter from the system, by first trapping it in a dedicated location (or several such locations), **and then cleaning those locations to remove the matter entirely from the tank and filters**.

Merely moving it from inside the tank, where you can see it floating around in the water, to the filters, does not improve the water quality at all. The only thing such achieves, is removing it from your sight, but not from the water. Leaving particulate matter trapped in the mechanical filters for too long does, in fact, more damage than good, as once the trapped matter is concentrated in a small area, it can quickly deplete large amounts of oxygen from the water. This material may then start decaying in an anaerobic (anoxic - oxygen poor or oxygen depleted) manner. This can quickly add many compounds that are totally undesirable, and dangerous, to the water . These compounds result from breakdown by-products. The better known one that you are probably familiar with is hydrogen sulfide, but there are many other such breakdown products that you do not want in the tank's water. Even small amounts of hydrogen sulfide lower the water quality enough, for your lifeforms not to look at their best.

Even if the decay that takes place does not remove all the oxygen (which it will in the extreme case), it can still remove considerable amounts, and lower dissolved oxygen to dangerous levels for all animal life you keep in the tank. They may not die, they will more than likely not, but they will just not look as good as they would, if the water quality were better.

It is all a matter of degree; the difference between a vibrant looking aquarium, and one that looks all right to you, but does not draw any oh's and ah's from your friends or visitors.

Mechanical filtration is, therefore, a two-step process : first you trap the dirt, detritus, floculate, particulate, (all names for what we are trying to remove) in a specially designed area by means of a screen, mesh, cartridge, floss, or other form of filter, and secondly you clean those filters regularly to remove that matter entirely from the system (the mass of water in your tank and filters). Doing so prevents whatever you trapped in the filters from breaking down, causing problems for you by lowering the water quality (usually evidenced by lower dissolved oxygen levels in the water). At the same time, because you prevented the decay, you also prevented the addition of other compounds that result from such decay, to the tank's water.

Some of these breakdown compounds may even be more toxic than the particulate matter that you trapped to begin with, obviating the need to clean your mechanical filters on a very regular basis. Once a week, or even more frequently, is strongly recommended.

Anything that can trap dirt acts as a mechanical filter, even materials in the tank and filters that you may not think about, e.g. the material used inside the trickle filter's biological filtration area (I am referring to material that is dense, close-meshed, or that packs and restricts the flow of the water, e.g. gravel).

Keep this in mind because, often, areas such as those never get cleaned, or they are cleaned much too infrequently. Examples are calcite layers in the bottom of filters, undergravel filters that are in dis-use or are used on a reduced flow rate, etc...

Mechanical filters come in many forms. They could be canisters filled with material such as EfiMech from Eheim, or Biomech from Kordon, filter floss, pads, blue-white bonded pads, bags; or they can be specially designed containers with pleated cartridges or bags, and many others still.

All work efficiently and will trap lots of detritus. The finer the material, the more it will remove, especially after it has accumulated some dirt already. As the spaces where the water can flow through get smaller, get restricted, finer and finer particles will be trapped. This will slow the flow of water through the material down as well, which is yet another reason why you should clean all such filters regularly.

Here is a short overview of the most common types of mechanical filtration methods used, and available to the Hobbyist. You should use at least one of them, but you may want to combine several in your system, for optimum efficiency.

■ Canisters (traditional) :

You probably know many of these filters under names such as Eheim, PEP, Lifeguard, Magnum, Fluval, Atlantis, Tech•, and assume that they all fall in the same category. That is not the case. Some are meant to be strictly mechanical filters, others can be adapted to perform several distinct functions: mechanical, chemical, biological, even heating, or a combination of several of those. The latter is what we would like to strongly discourage. **Segregate, don't combine. Keep all forms of filtration separate from each other.**

We must also differentiate between the traditional canister filters such as the Eheim, Fluval and Magnum types, and the others mentioned. The former can be loaded, or filled, with varying types of products, each one of which is meant to perform a different function. The latter are more of a pressure type filter, excellent at mechanical filtration.

In fish-only tanks that was certainly a very appropriate way of using these filters; in Reef tanks, we would like to discourage you from doing so (combining several filtration methods).

Remember, we are trying to keep all forms of filtration separate from each other, and since we will be using a trickle filter (see biological filtration), if you use a traditional canister, you should use it as either a mechanical or a chemical filter, not a combination.

Let's review how to use them as mechanical filters. Refer to the last section in this chapter to check up on chemical filtration canisters.

Canister filters have one great advantage : they can easily be opened and serviced. That is a boon ! **The easier it is to clean a filter, the more often the Hobbyist is likely to do so**. And cleaning the inside of mechanical filters often is a requirement, not an option, as we have already seen.

Fill your canister with any material that is available in your local area pet store, and that is meant to be used in a fine filter. Pack it in firmly, but not too tightly, lest you will restrict the water flow too much. Canister filters can move a fair amount of water, but their pumps do not usually take a lot of back pressure. Switch the canister on, and you will be mecha-nically filtering the water on a continuous basis. You can take water from the bottom of the trickle filter (sump), and return it to the same area, or you can return it to the tank directly, or to the top of the trickle filter. All three are acceptable. In-line mechanical filters are discussed later.

Many Hobbyists use filter floss, some use ceramic tubes such as EfiMech from Eheim (stands for efficient mechanical filtration), Kordon's equivalent : BioMech, pads such as blue-white bonded ones, coarse gravel, DLS or copy-cats of the original, foam sponges (beware though that most foam is bio-degradable, and if it is not, it may have been treated with compounds you do not want in your tank), natural sponges (my favorite), crushed coral, small coral rubble, Efigross (grob) a fine mesh of green plastic marketed by Eheim, layers of untreated viscose, and a host of other materials (hobbyists are very resourceful in this respect).

Clean the filter(s) at least once a week, more often is even better. Do not worry about bacterial loss, mechanical filters are not meant to act biologically. That is not their purpose. In fact, more often than not, the bacteria that grow in mechanical filters that are not regularly cleaned, do more harm than good, and some even suggest (de Graaf, 1976) that they may be the cause of wipe-outs, in some cases (Shigella type bacteria).

Cleaning the canister, *cum* mechanical filters, involves remov-ing all the material that you placed inside, and rinsing it thoroughly in fresh water before placing it back in the canister. Sometimes it even pays to use new material, e.g. in the case of filter floss. Some materials need to be scrubbed, others bleached. In the latter case make sure you rinse them several times to remove all bleach leftovers. Do not, if you can avoid it, use dechlorinators. I do not care for their use in Reef tanks.

In order to make this process as easy as possible, it is suggested that you use quick disconnect shut-off valves, on either side of the canister filter. This will allow you to take it out of service without having to worry about water spillage, except for the very little water that is between the canister and the quick disconnect valves.

Eheim, Fluval and Marineland make such valves, and there may be others. American made ones are as good as the imports, so my suggestion is that you save yourself the extra cost, as imported ones are usually more expensive, and not necessarily better.

The size of the canister should be in direct relation to the size of the system that you have. In most cases a Fluval 303, or perhaps a 403 for 55 gallon aquariums will be fine. This may be larger than what you expected, but you will benefit from the extra mechanical filtration ability that you will have. There are of course other brands; get the larger models if you can afford them, they will do a better job for you, as they hold more filtering material.

Eheim, probably the inventor of the canister filter, has recently introduced its 2200 series, very similar to the previous 2000 series, but with slightly more flow, and a normalized shaft. These top-of-the-line canisters are really good value for your money and hold up for years and years. I personally use Eheim 2217's whenever I need canister filters.

Filter floss is, in my opinion, just about as good as anything else you can find on the market. It is easy to use, relatively inexpensive, and can therefore be replaced each time you clean the filters. Buy it in bulk.

Make a habit of cleaning your canister(s) at least once a week. Your system will greatly benefit from it. That is my experience anyway. And if, as suggested, you use quick disconnect valves, cleaning and changing will not be a chore at all.

Remember, the easier it is to clean your mechanical

filter, the more often your are likely to do so, for the benefit of your system. I have said so for a very long time, and must remind you, that only when you first set up your tank, can you meaningfully influence this. Install all mechanical filters in a way that will let you reach them easily.

■ Canister filters (special)

Special canisters can be acquired to mechanically filter the water. Two examples are the PEP and Lifeguard Systems. These units usually require some piping, unlike the traditional canisters which the Hobbyist can just plug them in and run. Their installation is, however, not complicated, and if you already have them, by all means use them.

Most of these filters (there are others besides the two mentioned) use some form of pleated bag, or pleated device, to increase the amount of surface area through which the water can flow and be filtered. The more surface area, the better the filtration, of course.

The bags can be used as such, or special powders (often diatomaceous earth) can be added to the filter, to step the filtration up to very fine levels, in this case referred to a micronic.

Cleaning is a little more involved, as these bags usually need to be bleached to remove the accumulated detritus. This takes more time and requires that you make sure all the bleach is removed, before putting the bags, or other material, back in the canisters. It is, actually, a good idea to have an extra bag or pleated cartridge around. Especially so if your local pet shop does not normally carry them.

Because of the way they need to be cleaned, the pleated bags or cartridges will wear out. Make sure that whomever you buy such a unit from, if you decide to include this in your filtering system, will also be able to supply you with replacements. Some dealers don't, or you may have to special order them.

Although this type of filtration can be very efficient, it is, in my opinion, not a necessary expense on the smaller Reef Tank. However, if you have such a filter already, it is recommended that you use it anyway. They are indeed very efficient at removing even very fine particulate matter.

Some units come with pressure gauges. This allows you to determine when it is necessary to clean the cartridge (pleated bag or other device) based on what the manufacturer suggests. Indeed, increased levels of pressure inside the canister are an indication that it is plugged, and needs cleaning. Retro-fitting such pressure gauges is also possible.

If you plan to use one of these units, make sure that the pump that you will be using can handle the back pressure brought about by these filters. Small pumps will not do the job. Again, most manufacturers suggest which pump you should use.

Because canister filters are very versatile, some brands are offered in various configurations, e.g. heater modules, chemical modules, and of course, mechanical modules. Lifeguard and PEP are two examples.

Unless you already have one of them, we recommend an alternative way of fine filtration; less expensive than acquiring such units. Use either a canister, or check the section on trickle filters to see how fine filtering can be incorporated in the trickle filter itself. In fact, ideally, this option should be provided in the trickle filter you should get, either as an easy add-on option, or already built-in.

Special canisters, such as the ones described, come in various sizes, and if you plan on getting one, match the size up with what is recommended for your tank. Better still, buy one size larger. It can't hurt the system, and if you up-grade to a larger tank, you will probably already have the right size canister, and save yourself the extra expense of having to buy a new one. You may not be thinking about a larger tank right now, but believe me you will at some point. Most Hobbyists do.

Servicing will require that you shut your pump down, as these filters are usually piped in-line with the main water flow back to the tank. In fact, some tanks' filtration consists only of a series of these special canisters. Such may be efficient, but in a Reef set-up we do not recommend that you use such filtration as the only means of maintaining water quality. They can, as we have seen, be used as add-ons to the trickle filter, especially for mechanical and chemical filtration.

Shut-off valves should be placed on either side of these units, to allow for quick and easy opening and servicing. True union ball valves are probably the easiest type to use. Quick-disconnect shut-off valves are another possibility, and for most Hobbyists a less expensive way to go.

Piping in a by-pass line may be a worthwhile option, as it will allow you to service the filter without having to stop your system. To check how this is done, look at the drawing, a few pages ahead, in the section on molecular absorption filters and micron filters.

These type of special canster filters are often used in swimming pool and similar installations (e.g. spas). When shopping around for one, check your local pool places too. You may be able to get yourself a bargain. If you need fittings and plastic pipe, check the hardware stores, the do-it-yourself stores, and best of all, the local plumbing supply places. If you run out of options, U.S. Plastics, also called Industrial Plastics, in Lima, Ohio, sells by mail and has excellent prices.

■ Diatomaceous Earth Filters

Diatomaceous earth, the skeletons of diatoms, allows extremely fine filtering, usually down to 1 micron, a level at which many parasites are trapped as well.

This is very efficient filtering, but should, in my opinion, not be used too regularly on a Reef Tank, as it will filter out all of the free floating lifeforms that many filter feeders in your tank require for survival. Tanks always contain filter feeders, and depriving them of the food they require is not a sensible way to run such an aquarium.

If you use a Vortex Diatom, a Marineland, or a System 1 diatom filter, do so infrequently, and not for many many hours in a row. Use them to clean the water after you stir up the bottom, to remove particulate matter that is now floating around, and then clean the filter and put it away for a while. Regular use is, in my opinion not recommended.

Of course, in fish-only tanks they can be run continuously.

Suggestions have also been made that the use of diatomaceous earth may add silicates to the water (Thiel 1986, 1988).

That is undesirable insomuch as it may result in the appearance of live diatoms, which will make the tank look really unsightly. To demonstrate this fact, run water through a diatomaceous earth filter for a few hours, and test for silicate both before and after. You will be up for some real surprises.

Some of these filters can be used with "powdered" activated carbon as well. This is something to consider doing on an infrequent basis : once every 2 weeks, to once a month perhaps, to clean up the water chemically as well. Never use the diatom powder more than once. Clean the filter after each use and throw the powder away. If you let it sit in the filter, it will cake up, and anaerobic bacteria will appear within hours. When you then switch the unit back on, all the noxious compounds in the filter will enter your tank. A most dangerous situation that can lead to many problems, including massive die-offs !

Should you get such a filter for your Small Reef ? My own answer is no. The drawbacks are the filtering out of fine matter that filter filters need, and the possibility that silicates are added to the water and may give rise to live diatoms (for example Navicula, Berkeleya). If you happen to have one, use it very infrequently, and use the types that does not require diatomaceous earth. There are better ways of fine filtering the water that are more efficient.

■ Sand and Gravel Filters

Perhaps the best and certainly the least expensive to set up. A small old aquarium will do (if you don't have one, look in your local "bargain" newspaper in the pet section, you will find them advertised all the time).

The filter can be set up using a regular canister filter as well, filled with gravel (or sand, although it is probably better to use gravel.

Because sand is finer than gravel, sand filters will filter much finer material out of the water, but not as fine as to remove what your filter feeders need. Gravel is probably good enough and is easier to maintain and clean. Additionally it is unlikely that anaerobics will start in your gravel filter if you clean it regularly, and if water flows through it continuously.

You can use traditional canisters or special canisters, or you can build one yourself, using a acrylic tube that is outfitted with a top and a bottom. Since you will need to be able to access the inside to clean the filter, you must use some device that allows you to do so. A compression nut is usually best. Make sure it is all plastic, or if any metal is in contact with the salt water, it must be 316 SS. If it is not, you should coat it with some plastic liquid paint, or with aquarium silicone.

It is placed in the top or bottom of the cylinder and tightened. When the gravel (or sand) needs changing or cleaning, the cylinder can easily be opened, the filter material taken out, cleaned and placed back in the cylinder.

Although this type of filter may not be in wide use, it is one of the most efficient and also very inexpensive to construct or set-up. Remember to clean it regularly. You must remove the dirt that you ahve

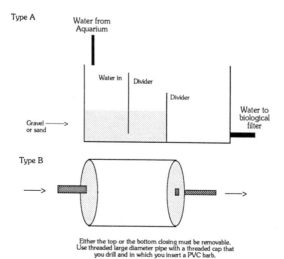

Either the top or the bottom closing must be removable.
Use threaded large diameter pipe with a threaded cap that
you drill and in which you insert a PVC barb.

trapped from the system (the total mass of water in the aquarium and what is in the sump of the filter, pipes, hose, etc.).

If you are not handy, or if you do not want to make the cylinder yourself, some can be obtained commercially. Alternatively, use the aquarium with divider method, shown in the diagram.

■ Micron and Sub-micron filters

Similar in their effect to the diatomaceous earth filters, micron and sub-micron filters are extremely efficient at cleaning up the water mechanically. They will remove even the smallest matter, especially if one uses the sub-micron (smaller than 1 micron) variety.

They often consist of a canister outfitted with a cartridge, or bag(s), that will not let particles through greater than the size the bag, or cartridge, is rated for, e.g. 5 microns, 1 micron, 0.65 micron etc... (see also diatomaceous earth filters which perform a similar type of filtration but use a different compound, and the reservations about using such filters expressed).

At that level of filtration even parasites are filtered out. Unfortunately so are all organisms and matter that your filter feeders feed on, and need. As already indicated this is not desirable. If you plan to use such a filter, use it only intermittently and not for extended periods of time.

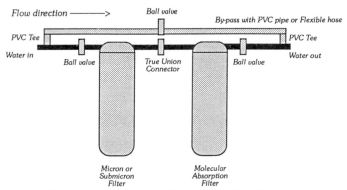

You can achieve the same results by using 2 canister filters
providing at least one of them has a micron filtering option

It is important to keep in mind also that such filters put a great deal of back pressure on the pump(s) and that you will lose more and more water flow, as the bag or cartridge loads itself with detritus.

Filters of this kind are rated in both nominal and absolute ratings. Nominal simply means that they will effectively remove **most** of the matter larger than what the filter is rated for, e.g. 90 percent or better. Absolute means that they remove **all** matter larger than the rating. As you can well imagine the second variety is quite a bit more expensive than the first.

Several standard canister filters can be outfitted with special inserts that act as micron filters. This usually does not make it necessary for most Hobbyists to buy a special unit.

The better ones, however, are filters specifically built for the purpose of micronic filtration. One such example is the Poly-Bio-Marine PSM-1 filter, which can easily be installed in line, and used in conjunction with the PMA-1 filter, the molecular absorption type (see Chemical filtration for more explanations on that type of filtration).

If you install a micron or sub-micron filter in-line, you should pipe it in such a way, that it can be by-passed, by switching valves. This will allow you to run the system without the micron (sub) filters for most of the time, and run the filters only when you want to, for short periods of time.

By leaving the valves that control the "in" and "out" to the fine filters slightly open, you will allow some water to go through all the time. This will prevent the formation of anaerobic activity in those canisters. It is even used by some to function as a denitrating filter. When doing so, you must make the water flow through the canister/filter, very slowly.

Since you will also have to be able to clean the filter, you will need a total of three valves to perform this. The illustration clearly shows how to pipe such a system, either with hard pvc pipe, or with acrylic or flexible pvc hose (better).

If you are not sure how to do so, check with someone who does, or call somone in the Hobby you know who can explain to you how to set such a system up.

These filters put a great deal of strain and back pressure on the pump(s) you are using. It is, therefore, a good idea to plan for a pump that can handle that pressure, when setting up the system.

These filters only make sense in a small Reef aquarium if you happen to have one already. I do not recommend it as a integral part of a basic set-up. Save yourself the expense. And if you do decide to buy one, get a good quality unit. The PSM is probably the best you can get and the easiest to service.

■ Miscellaneous

Mechanical filters can be made using any convenient container and filter floss or gravel, or a combination of both. This is easy to achieve if you are using a trickle filter at the same time, as all you will need to do is first flow the water into that container, and through the media, and then from that container to the top of the trickle filter.

A old aquarium, or a plastic bucket if that is all you have, will do just fine, and will make the filter quite inexpensive. In fact, if you refer to some old FAMA magazines, in the For What it's Worth column, you will find many suggestions on how to set such filters up.

Without a trickle filter (see biological filtration) it is very difficult to use this form of mechanical filter, unless float switches (level switches) are used as well. This complicates the set-up and can increase its price quite a bit.

One tried method that is often inexpensive to install, consists of using old canister filters, place them in series, and run them with an old pump you have sitting around. Not the pumps that came with the canisters, but something stronger than that as, to push water forcefully through one or more canister filters, you may need something the equivalent of a Number 2 or 3 magnetic drive pump (brands include Little Giant, March, Iwaki, and others). Do not use extra strong pumps as the canisters will not take a very high amount of inside pressure.

If you do not own such a pump, look in your local "bargains" advertisement paper, ask the Pet stores you deal with for second hand pumps, or call other Pet Stores in your area. Your local Aquarium Society may also be a good source for getting equipment you need.

■ Mechanical Filter in Syphon :

To bring water down to a trickle filter two methods are used. Either the surface skimming syphon arrangement, or holes in the tank combined with a corner overflow box (see The Marine Fish and Invert Reef Aquarium for a detailed discussion).

A number of syphon devices have a pre-filter (mechanical filter) built in to the downflow. That is of course an excellent way of filtering the water, as it is done one step before the water enters the biological part of the trickle filter, thus reducing the amount of detritus that can get stuck there. This is especially important with certain types of materials used in such filters, e.g. DLS and similar materials that go by different names.

The latter, due to its denseness, can indeed trap dirt very easily. Such is totally undesirable, as it will quickly lead to reduced levels of dissolved oxygen, which, as we shall see later, will stress all tank life, and lead to a system that is not running at its optimum, and in which disease and micro-algae will more than likely occur intermittently or, more likely, all the time.

Mechanical filters inside syphons are usually made of coarse foam that traps the dirt. Clean it regualarly. At least once a week. Remove the sleeve, or twist it loose (as in the Smit's Natural Reef model and also in a few others), rinse it out, and place it back in the syphon.

❏ **Conclusion :**

■ You must clean the water with a mechanical filter, and you should do so before the water enters the biological filter.

■ You must clean the mechanical filter(s) regularly, at least once a week. More often can not hurt, to the contrary.

■ You should, in my opinion, not use micronic, sub-micronic and diatomaceous earth filters on small Reef tanks, and if you do, you should only use them very infrequently.

■ The denser the material inside your biological filter contact chamber, the more importance mechanical filtration of the water going to that filter, before it gets there, becomes. Indeed, this will prevent dirt getting trapped too quickly, loss of dissolved oxygen and decay inside the biological filter.

■ Several mechanical filters, instead of just one, do not hurt the system, on the contrary, but are, in my opinion not a requirement. They just add to the cost of setting up the tank, unless of course you have them standing around anyway.

■ A complete trickle filter with all the required types of filtration incorporated, and segregated, is the ideal system to go with for a small Reef Aquarium.

■ How such a filter is built and what it looks like may not be what you have in mind right now. The traditional box-like filters that have been around for several years are obviously one way to go, but there are other approaches that we will discuss.

Look for our recommendations on mechanical filtration later in this book. You may also wish to refer to the How To section of FAMA magazines, as many ways of fine filtering have been described there.

Incidentally, FAMA published all the HOW TO's in book form. Check with them for ordering information. FAMA is the abbreviation for Freshwater and Marine AQUARIUM magazine.

■ Biological Filtration

■ General Remarks

What biological filtration is all about, is not the subject matter of this book. You may wish to refer to general marine aquarium books if you are not entirely familiar with biological filtration, or if you want to read up on it some more.

One not-general-at-all book, but a very detailed one on marine aquarium systems that we highly recommend is "The Marine Aquarium Reference-Systems and Invertebrates", by Martin Moe, 1989. It contains a wealth of information that you will be interested in, as well as many practical tips and advice that you will be able to put to good use. Besides that, it explains a lot of the more theoretical concepts in clear language, understandable by the average Hobbyist.

Biological filtration is a very important component of your total filtration system. As most of you know, breakdown products of metabolism and decay of protein, produce either ammonium ion or ammonia depending on the pH of the medium .

In a marine environment where the pH is relatively high, a percentage of this ammonium ion is in the form of ammonia, a very soluble and toxic gas. Even very small amounts of NH_3 are extremely toxic and will cause great stress to the fish and invertebrates, killing some of them off, which creates more pollution and more stress.

To remove this ammonia and ammonium ion nature, comes to our help with the nitrification process, whereby ammonia is converted to nitrite, and nitrite to nitrate by bacteria that will grow spontaneously in the tank, or that can be added (seeding) when first starting up the tank, to speed up their proliferation.

Bacteria grow everywhere, not just in a biological filter. Please keep that in mind. The size of the bacterial population is also determined by the amount of nutrient available to them. Keep that in mind too. Most Hobbyists do not, and think that once their filter is cycled, they can put a large number of fish and invertebrates in the tank, without danger, and immediately.

That is not so ! It is a mistake very often made, and it leads to die-offs, disease, stress, and a host of problems. Look at it this way : a biological filter that is very potent during the cycle, can only keep sustaining the same amount of pollution as it had during the cycle. If you increase the load in the tank to beyond that level, the filter has to re-adjust and build up even more bacteria.

To simplify the explanation : if you had 5 pieces of so-called live rock in the tank during the first 4 weeks (i.e.during the cycle), and it required, for argument's sake, 7 million bacteria to cope with the pollution so generated, you cannot expect those same 7 million bacteria to cope with 10 pieces of live rock (keep in mind that the numbers are arbitrary and bear no relationship to the real numbers. They are only used to illustrate a point).

To cope with this new load you will need even more bacteria. They will grow spontaneously in your filter, but it will take a few days for them to appear and neutralize the increased amound of ammonia (and subsequently the higher amount of nitrite).

Each time you add an animal or an invertebrate, more ammonia is generated and more bacteria are necessary in the filter to neutralize that pollution. That is the reason for the often found recommendation : add new tank inhabitants only a few at a time, and wait several days between each introduction (your safest bet is to check for ammonia and nitrite, if none is found you can add more lifeforms).

Indeed, doing so let's the filter catch up (meaning more bacteria grow) without creating undue stress on the animal life already in the tank. This results in a safe and gradual increase in the tank's population. If, in addition, you use the recommended methods for adding fish and inverts, you should not have any problems with outbreaks of parasitic infestations.

No one can offers 100 percent guarantees, but if you follow these recommendations, your chances of not getting any parasites will be greatly improved. You are, then, also less likely to lose the animals (and the money they cost you). Marine Reef, the newsletter, featured several articles on this subject already.

A similar remark applies to biological filters that are started up with several rocks or fish, and then left to run with far less lifeforms for a while. The filter adjusts to the lower amount of pollution. If the Hobbyist then decides to place a larger number of lifeforms in the tank again, the filter will not be able to cope with this increased load. It will need to re-adjust first, and that takes time. If you do not let the filter adjust, stress will be created and lifeforms will be lost (or as often is the case, disease will break out).

This is an important remark to remember with regard to biological filters ! How long the re-adjustment phase will take cannot be predicted. Testing for ammonia and nitrite is the only sure way to determine whether or not the filter is ready for an increased load. Both should test zero ppm (or mg/l).

We noted that mechanical filtration is important for two reasons :
❏ it removes particulate matter before it can break down and pollute the water,
❏ it makes the tank look more appealing, by unclouding the water and removing debris.

Correct biological filtration is very important because it :
❏ breaks down ammonia to nitrite (Nitrosomonas bacteria)
❏ breaks down nitrite to nitrate (Nitrobacter bacteria)
❏ oxygenates the water for the benefit of all lifeforms and the filter itself.
❏ removes a number of unwanted compounds through facultative aerobic-anaerobic activity in portions of the filter (Wolff 1984).

Incidentally, and as a reminder that trickle filters are not some recent development, the first reference to such filters that I could find is in a book published in 1935, yes that long ago, called American Sewerage Practice, by Leonard Metcalf and Harrisson Eddy, Volume 3 of 3, The Maple Press Company, York, Penna. Call them if you are

interested in how large volumes of water get treated. That book was brought to my attention by Matthew Cammarata.

The filters in that book are large, some even very large, at least compared to what we use in the Hobby nowadays, but the principle behind their efficiency has not changed an iota over the years.

Such biological filters (not necessarily all trickle filters) can be set up in many ways. All work of course, or Hobbyists would not have used them for several years now, and they would not be around in the literature anymore.

There are however varying degrees of efficiency in the types, brands and models available on the market. Some just do a better job than others. You know most of them :

         ❑ Canister filters, traditional
         ❑ Canister filters, special

❑ Undergravel filters, regular flow, reverse flow
❑ Outside box filters
❑ Trickle filters in many configurations
❑ and a combination of one or more of the above.

There are other types of biological filters too, perhaps not as familiar to you, but they are used by a fair number of Hobbyists too:

❑ BioMesh filters
❑ Ruecksack or Backpack filters (hang-on trickle filters)
❑ Tray Filters, similar to trickle filters
❑ Outside the tank biological sand filters
❑ and a variety of intermediate ones, based on the sand filter system.

All of them serve the same purpose : the three reasons stated above. As indicated, however, some of these filters do a much better job than others at improving water quality, especially where it comes to re-oxygenating the tank's water.

Years in the hobby, especially in Europe, the trickle filter has made great strides in this country too. In 1985, when I first imported trickle filters from Germany (from a company called Nollman Aquaristik, in Sennestadt), hardly anybody even knew what such filters looked like, or what they were supposed to do. Nowadays, just looking at the ads in the Hobby magazines, everyone seems to claim "they" were the first to ever offer this type of filter (refer too to my earlier remark about the 1935 reference to trickle filters in "American Sewerage Practice" to convince yourself that such is merely advertising copy).

Who was the first, and when, is not important and germane, what counts is that these filters are extremely efficient, and that for the purpose we are interested in - high quality water - they are the foremost filter, and the most effective at the present time. The variety and number of such filters now available attests to their success, and to the fact that both manufacturers, and Hobbyists alike, believe in them.

Because I strongly believe that to run a successful Reef you need such a filter, or a similar type e.g. a hang-on unit (Ruecksack or some types of conversion units, for instance), we will review only such filters in this section. Information on undergravel, and similar filters, can be found in many other books, as I am sure you are aware of. Refer to them if you still want more details, or if you want to review and compare them with trickle filtration.

■ General principles of Trickle Filtration :

Inside an appropriate compartment, a medium is placed on which *Nitrosomonas* and *Nitrobacter* can grow in large numbers. The shape of the box has absolutely no bearing whatsoever on the efficiency of the filter, although most manufacturers make them square or rectangular, because round tube or pipe of the size usually required, would make the filter much more expensive.

When dealing with the shape of a trickle filter, the important factors to take into account are the following, in my opinion:

❏ filters that are too narrow tend to create "channeling" of the water against the outside panels of the filter, resulting in very inefficient use of the medium,
❏ filters that are short, meaning not tall enough, do not promote re-oxygenation very well, and are therefore not as desirable. The minimum sugested height of the column of biological medium is 12 to 14 inches.

Most filters you see are clear, probably because clear acrylic is less expensive than other varieties. In fact, the filter would do better if it was not clear, as the bacteria perform better in the dark (documented in too many articles to mention). Nollman Aquaristik, of Sennestadt Germany, which has been building filters for many more years than anyone in the USA, builds theirs in opaque PVC sheet. Luebbecke Aquarium who have used large trickle filters on their 10.000+ gallon system for many years, uses 3 foot diameter grey PVC pipeline sections.

Another reason may be that clear filters can easily be looked into, something the Hobbyist likes to do, to determine how the water is flowing through the medium.

The biological filter compartment should be removable from the other parts of the filter. This allows for easier transport and shipping, easier installation, and much easier cleaning of the other parts of the filter when the need arises (and it will, believe me, mainly because most filters on the market do not have slanted bottoms which will require you to syphon out detritus from time to time).

As the water comes down from the tank to the filter, and disperses inside the biological chamber, it travels over the medium and allows the bacteria that grow on them to polish the water by first converting ammonia to nitrite (one type of bacterium) and then from nitrite to nitrate (another bacterium).

The better the dispersion of the water, the better the water is spread over the medium, and the better the filter will be able to clean up the water. That should be obvious. Not only is filtration more efficient, but by using the medium more efficiently you will need less of it. This can save you quite a few dollars as most of the media are still relatively expensive.

Additionally, less medium fits in a smaller filter, and that too will

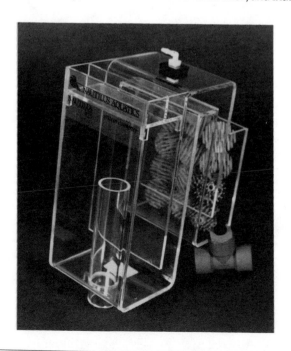

save you money. It will also make more space available underneath the aquarium, and since space there is at a premium....

Because you do not want to have to clean the biological filter - in doing so you would destroy a large amount of bacteria - the medium should allow a good throughflow of water, and not trap dirt that may have slipped through your fine filters (mechanical filtration). It is'nt supposed to, but some will. If it gets stuck in the medium, in the long run you are looking at cleaning it. We already stated that such is not desirable at all.

Dense material will plug up no matter how well you filter. The main reasons for this is that fine particular matter not trapped in the fine filters will eventually clog certain areas of your dense biological filter, creating anoxic pockets. When oxygen levels are low, or non-existent, decay is proceeding anaerobically, and hydrogen sulfide is produced. This will pull your water quality down very quickly.

In fact, if you were measuring redox potential levels, and they are low, even though you are using a considerable amount of ozone, the likely reason is that small amounts of hydrogen sulfide are pulling the redox down, because of the reductive power of hydrogen sulfide. Increasing the ozone may not even help. You must eliminate the H_2S to bring the redox potential back up. There exist of course many other reasons for low redox potential, some of them will be covered elsewhere in this book, especially in the *Maintenance Section*.

■ Components of a good Trickle Filter :

We already mentioned the biological compartment. Several features of this compartment are important, because they add to the efficiency on one hand, and to the ease of installation and servicing on the other :

❏ Because acrylic warps easily when in contact with water, good reinforcements of the side of the biological compartment are very

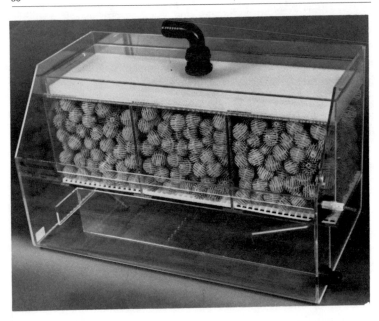

desirable. Beware of filters made out of very thin acrylic or similar materials. They will warp, and may split on you, unless reinforcements have been added to prevent this from happening.

❏ A removable lid is a plus. Dirt will get into the top of the filter whether you like it or not. When the lid at the top is removable, it will be very easy for you to remove that dirt. The lid should also be reinforced, or made out of glass (best). If you can't get to the top, the dirt will do two things : it will decay and reduce water quality, and it will plug up holes in the drip plate (if that is what you are using, and you should).

❏ At least two air inlets are recommended. The bacteria inside the filter are aerobic, meaning that they require oxygen to perform. Blowing a good flow of air into the filter is therefore very desirable. The better the air is spread out, the better the filter will operate. I usually recommend that Hobbyists use a air pump such as a Whisper 1000, or stronger (e.g. Wisa), and blow all the air inside the biological chamber, using both the air inlets. If only one is available, you may wish to drill a second one, push airline tubing through it, and then pack a little aquarium silicone around the hole, so no water comes out. Blowing more air will not hurt, to the contrary. To convince yourself of the benefit of doing this, run air into the biological chamber, note the redox potential, now shut off the air, and then watch what happens to the redox potential: it will go down (Bepko, 1988, Thiel, 1988). It may even go down quite a bit. You must blow the air into the chamber above the water level, directly into the column, not through an airstone placed in the water underneath the biological chamber.

❏   The height of the chamber should be at least 12 to 14 inches. Shallower filters will work, but you will need to flow more water through them. Because there really is a limit to how much water can be flowed through a small biological chamber. Excessive current through the filter will wash off some of the bacteria, and result in a less efficient filter, less oxygenation, and a smaller biological colony.

❏ The width of the chamber should be no less than 8 inches. Narrower filter chambers channel too much water on the sides rather than through and over the medium used, and that reduces the efficiency of the filter.

❏ Use a filter with a drip plate rather than a spray bar. The reasons for this are explained in the section on drip plates, later in this section.

❏ The chamber should not sit too deeply in the sump. This will keep all the medium out of the water in the sump. Bacterial beds that are out of the water are more efficient at handling ammonia and nitrite. Wolff (1984) suggests that the efficiency goes down to less than 60 percent when the medium is submersed.

❏ Larger sumps are to be preferred. They increase the total volume of water in the the system, and make it easier for you to use a powerful pump. If too little water is in the sump, evaporation will lower its level quickly, and if, as you should, you are using a float switch, the pump will stop regularly, and eventually altogether when the water level is real low.

Larger sumps also have more space for other devices that you may want to add to your system and that you may wish to run with a power head

❏   The sump should preferably be reinforced too, as this will prevent warping and possibly splitting months down the road.

❏   Compartments built-in the sump are always a plus. They allow you to easily add certain compounds to the system. Make sure however that the compartments are built in such a way that the water coming from the biological chamber *must* flow through them, not just over them. Whatever you place in them will work better if the water has to go through the compound completely

❏   Depending on the size of the tank, you will be using a particular pump. Check the in and outlet sizes of the pump. Make sure the hole in the filter is of the same size, or larger, than the size of the pump intake. Re-drilling an existing hole is not the easiest and safest thing to do. If a bulkhead fitting is already included you will not have to go out an buy one. If you do, buy a real tank fitting, not a rigged male/female fitting type arrangement.

❏   Built-in foam fractionators - protein skimmers are a definite plus, but they must be of the size that your system requires. Not some flimsy little skimmer that was built to fit the filter rather than the tank ! This is most important because undersized skimmers will be a real problem for the tank, and are one of many reasons for the appearance of red algae. See the section on skimmers for more details on sizing. Don't lull yourself into thinking that you have one if the filter you bought has a real small skimmer built into it. Stick with either an outside columnar one, or a built-in Venturi skimmer, and make sure that you can use ozone with it, because you probably will want to, or need to.

❏   A sump with a slanted bottom will allow mulm and other detritus from being moved forward by the current, making it much easier for you to syphon it out. Mind you, mulm is technically speaking inert, and should not affect the water quality any longer, it is the detritus that needs to be removed.

❏   Certain filters have a built-in tray for electrodes. That is handy if you are using them, but in the basic system that we are setting up, we will not.

❑ Whether the sump has a lid, or not, does not really make much of a difference. Most of the evaporation is not from the sump, but from the aquarium itself. It makes the filter look more finished though.

■ Sizing the Trickle Filter :

From an economics standpoint this is a most important section. Buy a filter that is too large and you spend more money on the filter and also on the internal medium. Buy one that is too small, and your water quality will suffer, and you may lose fish, invertebrates, and ultimately money too.

In my estimation, buying the wrong filter will end up costing you two to three hundred dollars more than you should have spent. Of

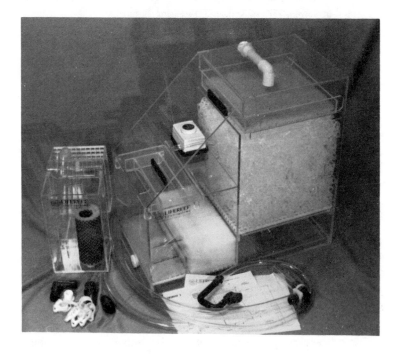

course, building your own filter would be the least expensive way to go. Plans are available in the magazines, and were also published in my other books.

The ultimate size of the filter will largely depend on the internals (biological medium) you use. The better the medium, the less of it you will need, and the smaller the filter will become as a result.

Here are my suggestions for sizing, providing you use either Bio•Techs, or Bio Blocks. Both are available from dealers nationwide, and cost about the same per gallon volume of the material.

- Tanks up to 40 gallons : you will need 4 gallons of internals.
- Tanks up to 55 gallons : use any trickle filter that can hold 4.5 gallons of the above materials.
- Tanks up to 70 gallons : you will need a filter that can hold 6 gallons of biological filtering medium.
- Tanks up to 110 gallons : 7.5 gallons of capacity required.
- Tanks 125 - 135 gallons : 8.5 gallons of internals needed.
- Tanks 150 gallons : 10 gallons .

The above numbers are lower than what you normally will find recommended because they are based on tests, not on advertising claims made by various manufacturers of plastic filtering media.

They assume you follow the directions in this book : most importantly that good dispersion is achieved by means of a "drip plate" of the kind we describe. This means that you may have to slightly modify (easy and explained later) the drip plate that comes with the filter you have bought, or are using now.

➡ Why are these recommendations lower ? Over the last 5 years I have had the opportunity to personally use the following media: German blue balls, Jaeger Tri-Packs (2 sizes), Bio Cubes, Bio•Techs, Pall Rings, Norton Rings, Plastic haircurlers, EfigroB, Raschig rings, Bio Discs, Cut PVC pipe, Cut acrylic chips, Gravel trays, Sand trays, Beads, Dolomite, and others still.

Doing so gives one a pretty good experience with which materials provide the kind of filtration required for Marine Reef tanks, and allows for fair and educated comparisons of their respective merits.

The following criteria guided me in deciding which internal plastic medium to use myself, and recommend to others :

> ✓ Dissolved oxygen levels after all ammonia and nitrite was converted.
> ✓ Speed at which ammonia was converted to nitrite and,
> ✓ Speed at which nitrite was converted to nitrate,
> ✓ Gaseous exchanges : e.g. was the CO_2 level within the norm?
> ✓ Do they trap dirt, how much, and what size ?
> ✓ Once dirt is trapped, how long does it stay in the filter ?
> ✓ Does water flow evenly, continuously, over the medium ?
> ✓ Does channeling occur, and if so, do what degree ?

→ Does the material you are using stack up ?

We have not recommended a product called pax, because it seems to trap more detritus than we feel is safe for your system. Unless some modifications to that material are made we feel that it is not a "best buy" for Reef tanks. It does well for fish-only tanks however. Biological filtration in Reef Tanks requires attention to details, not just "surface area" or "dispersion ability". Select what you buy very carefully.

■ Important Media Considerations :

The following qualities are important considerations when buying internal plastic biological filtration materials (usually Polyethylene, or plastic, as it is generally referred to) :

✔ the material should not trap dirt and debris. This includes pieces of food, algae, and any other free floating particulate matter.

✔ the material should allow good gaseous exchange by braking up the water in really fine streams and drops.

✔ the material should have a relatively large surface area. You will need somewhere between 2 and 2.5 square feet of biological filtration area per gallon of water in the tank. The exact amount, whether the lower number or not, depends on the load in the tank. If the distribution of the water over the medium is really maximized, you can go as low as 1.25 square feet of surface area per gallon of water.

    ✔ the material should be totally inert. No leachings whatsoever are allowed.

    ✔ the material should maximize the utilization of the biological chamber. This means that there should not be large gaps between the individual media pieces.

    ✔ the material should be permanent, meaning that it does not deteriorate, and thus never needs replacing.

    ✔ the material should be unbreakable, so that no rods, or pieces, break off and ruin the pump impellers and volute, and possibly the inside of a chiller, if you were to use one (not part of a basic system of course).

    ✔ it should not be too rough as that would result in dead bacteria being overgrown by live colonies, which is not desirable as it will lead to very small amounts of anaerobic activity underneath the live active layer, possibly killing some of the live layer of bacteria off, or reducing its potency due to anaerobic activity by-products (Thiel, 1988).

■ Drip Plate or Spray Bar ?

The controversy surrounding this topic has been going on for quite some time now. Very simply, it is my educated opinion, based on extensive testing, that drip plates perform better in trickle fiters than spray bars do, because :

    → they distribute the water more evenly,

    → contain dissolved gasses better, and

    → are not subject to clogging ,

    → and slowing down, the way spray bars are.

We, therefore, now recommend drip plates in trickle filters, and have, after trying many variations, arrived at the drip plate that we feel performs best :

    → Hole size of 3/16"

    → Holes separated by 3/4 inch spaces,

    → Plate grooved for better water distribution,

    → Hole size commensurate with flow rate,

    → Holes tapered at the top of the place.

    → No holes within 1 inch of all filter sides, to reduce channeling

You can modify an existing drip plate by plugging holes that are too close to the sides with aquarium silicone, and add holes if necessary. If the plate can be removed you can do so rather easily, if not, you must drill the plexiglass plate while leaving it where it is. Use only acrylic drill bits ! *They will prevent cracking of the acrylic when you drill through it.* They are not expensive, and are sold at most stores that sell acrylic in custom cut sizes.

To position the holes correctly, draw lines with an acrylic scratching tool, 3/4" apart length wise, and 3/4" apart cross wise. Then drill holes where the lines cross (see drawing below).

To obtain tapered holes, use a small countersink drill bit after you have drilled the holes. This gives the tapered effect which will im-

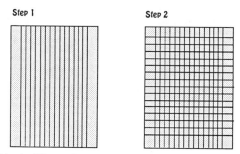

Holes should be spaced equidistant in both directions. Half inch is suggested

prove the flow of the water downwards into the biological chamber, and over distribute it better over the medium you are using.

Although the drip plate may not appear to you as a significant part of the trickle filter, it is a very important one. Indeed, by selecting the correct one, or modifying it as we suggested, you can ensure a much more even dispersion of the water coming down from the tank, over the medium that you are using.

That in itself assures a more efficient biological filtration and, ultimately, a greatly improved water quality, the purpose of using a trickle filter to begin with.

■ Retrofitting for a slanted bottom :

Most units on the market have a "flat" trickle filter bottom. As we have seen, this does not promote the forward moving of detritus and debris. Retrofitting an existing filter is not complicated at all :

❶ Measure the inside dimensions of the sump very carefully. The match of the plate you will be adding, with the inside of the sump must be exact. Measure from the back of the filter, coming towards the front, up to where the biological chamber ends. The plate only needs to be long enough to fit underneath the biological chamber.

❷ Acquire the piece of acrylic from a plastic dealer in your area.

❸ Place the plate in the sump in such a way that it slants forward at an angle of a few degrees only.

❹ Dry the sides where you will need to glue properly. This is really important because glue does not stick if the sides are still moist. Go over the sides of the filter with paper towels several times.

❺ Use aquarium silicone to glue the plate in place. Glue with care because you need a very good seal. No water can be allowed to get underneath the plate. It would stagnate and create anaerobic conditions.

❻ Let dry for at least 75 minutes, preferably somewhat longer. Since not a great deal of pressure will be exerted on the seams you glued, you will not need a 24 hours curing period.

⮑ The force of the current over the slanted plate will now move the debris and detritus forward, and you will be able to syphon it out very easily. In the process you will prevent it from decaying in the system and reduce your dissolved oxygen levels.

■ Adding Compartments to the Sump :

Rather than buying canister filters to add certain water filtering products to your tank, you may wish to add compartments to hold these same compounds.

Included in this list of compounds are, for instance, X-nitrate, Poly Filters, molecular absorption discs, resins for chemical filtrations, and others.

- ◆ decide on the size of the compartment you will add,
- ◆ measure the exact dimensions of the acrylic pieces needed,
- ◆ obtain the pieces and make sure you have enough silicone sealer,
- ◆ use any one of the two designs below to build your compartment,
- ◆ place the compartment in the filter, and add the compound.

Type 1 : *Place the unit off the bottom of the filter by resting it on a ledge made of small blocks on all corners. For most efficient set up glue the corners onto the compartment. Use acrylic cement, or*

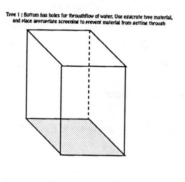

Type 1 : Bottom has holes for throughflow of water. Use eggcrate type material, and place appropriate screening to prevent material from getting through

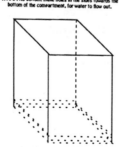

Type 2 : No bottom. make holes in the sides towards the bottom of the compartment. for water to flow out.

aquarium silicone. Place floss or screening on the bottom to prevent the material from getting through.

Type 2

No base (bottom). The compartment rests on the bottom of the sump. Drill holes all around the base to let the water get out easily.

Quarter inch holes usually will do. **Remark :** *Clean the material regularly to prevent it from clogging and restricting the water flow.*

Remember to change the material that you are using in these compartments on a regular basis. Most exhaust themselves as they do what they are meant to do. Follow the manufacturer's instructions in this respect.

If you do not attach (glue) the compartments permanently to the base of the sump, you will be able to remove them, and replace them with a larger (or smaller) one, should the need for that arise. Not attaching them will also simplify cleaning them, as all you will have to do is remove it (them). Always remove them very slowly, to prevent detritus trapped inside from getting into the sump of the trickle filter, and being sucked in by the pump(s).

■ Fittings on the trickle filter :

❑   A good trickle filter should come equipped with all fittings needed to hook it up.

❑   This includes a fitting a the top, a hook-up for airline tubing, and one where the pump needs to be attached.

❑   It does not include ball valves and check valves, neither does it include float switches and the like, except perhaps in the top-of-the-line units.

❑   If the filter has a skimmer built-in, a hook-up for that should be provided as well. Again, make sure that the skimmer can be used with ozone if you are planning to do so, and that it is placed in such a way, that flowing the outcoming water over carbon is easy.

It should also not allow air-ozone from getting into the back compartment where your biological medium is, as ozone will destroy the bacteria in the biological filter.

❑ To save on the total height, look for a filter that has a 90 degree angled fitting for the water inlet at the top.

■ Float Switches :

There are many uses in the Hobby for float switches. Level control is an important feature of a modern aquarium, and you should certainly consider adding it to your tank, especially since inexpensive models have now become available.

Keep in mind that water levels can be controlled in various ways
→ prevent water from getting too low,
→ prevent water from rising too high,
→ or a combination of both, using double switches.

Float switches that control the "low" do two main things for your system's stability and protection :
→ They prevent the pump from running dry when the water level in the sump gets reduced because of evaporation, or when you remove water yourself, for whatever purpose you may do so (for example when changing water).
→ They even out (balance out) the amount of water going up to the tank, and the amount coming down to the filter as, if the level in the sump drops too much (you regulate the height at which the float switch triggers) because more is going up than coming down, the float goes down, and stops the pump for a short period, until the level in the sump goes back up.

Float switches that control the "high" serve the following purposes :
→ add from a reserve vat. When the level in the sump reaches the desired level (which you decide on) the float shuts the pump that is adding water down, remotely. Indeed, the pump is in the reserve vat, the float switch is in the sump, and senses the level as it goes up.
→ shut down a solenoid valve that controls water coming a large skimmer to the sump, for instance. You are unlikely to use this feature in a basic system, however, because of the high cost of setting this up. A large and reliable solenoid (e.g. 1 inch in and outlet) costs close to $ 450.00.

When in the market for a float switch, shop around ! You should consider the following types that are commonly available:

- Reed switches
- Mercury switches
- Infra-red switches

All have advantages and disadvantages :

- Reed switches are inexpensive, but harder to install, and may require that you operate them via a special relay. This does not make them very practical for the average Hobbyist to use.
- Mercury switches are more expensive. They are extremely reliable, but can be rather bulky and are not as easy to find. Installation is not difficult, but will take a little more time.
- Infra-red switches are very reliable, cost even more, but are extremely easy to install. If you are considering this type make sure that it can sense through the scuzz that builds up on the side of the trickle filter sump. Of course, they only work with transparent filters.

The key when using float switches, is to make them trigger at the correct level. With mercury and infra-red switches this is real easy, with reed switches it is a little more complicated and time consuming.

The trigger point should always be at least 1.5 inches above the top of the intake hole of the pump. This to prevent air from being sucked into the pump because of a vortex that will form around the intake area, if the level in the sump is too low.

Air in the pump volute and impeller area, makes the pump run much hotter, and heats up the water too. Additionally the air may be broken up by the impeller, and extremely small bubbles may form. These are pushed into the tank, making it look real unsightly. Such small bubbles can also cause nitrogen gas bubble disease.

Small, reliable, float switches can often be obtained from Marine Supply companies and shops. They are usually operated in conjunction with bilge pumps on boats. Make sure that they have no metal parts that can come in contact with the water in your sump, except if the metal is 316 SS. Additionally, they must be made to run on 110 volts, not 12 or 24 volts.

■ Hard Piping or Flexible Hose ?

Although many Hobbyists prefer hard pvc pipe for all the hook-ups and connections, flexible hose is just as good and reliable. Additionally, if you source the flexible hose from a discount supplier, you will save quite a bit of money.

You will still need ball valves and check valves, of course, but you can mail order those from companies such as U.S. Plastics in Lima, Ohio, or other ones that advertise in the aquarium magazines. Alternatively, get them from a local plumbing supply house, or from swimming pool places. Shop around ! Prices can vary tremendously, as some of you may have found out.

Hard piping requires that you familiarize yourself with how to glue PVC pipe together, and also which fittings will do the job you are trying to accomplish. Check the Marine Fish and Invert Reef Aquarium book, the chapter on Fittings, if you are not familiar with them.

Flexible hose installations are usually simpler to perform, quicker to finish, but do not look as "tidy". Remember to always use hose clamps wherever you join flexible hose to an instrument, a device, or to pvc pipe and plastic fittings. This is most important to prevent leaks, and ensure that the hose will not slip off as a result of the internal pressure building up inside the system. If that happens to you, you will have a lot of water on the floor !

■ Fittings other than on the filter :

You will need at least one ball valve and at least one check valve per water line running back to the aquarium, to ensure that your system is totally safe.

The ball valve will allow you to adjust the water flow going back to the tank from the filter, preventing too great a flow, and the check valve will prevent back syphoning through the line running up to the tank, should the pump break down, or should a power failure occur. More details can be found in my other two books as well.

Shop around for these and other valves you may be using, as mark-ups vary widely from dealer to dealer, even from plumbing supply place to plumbing suply place.

Place the ball valve about 1 foot away from the output of the pump (see diagram). Place the check valve either inside the trickle filter, or between the filter and the system's main pump.

If you place the check valve inside the sump, right on the pump intake, you will be able to prime the pump (getting the air out) much faster and in an easier manner. When you do so, you should cover the intake side of the check valve with a special screen, which converts the check valve to a so-called foot valve.

Installation of Valves

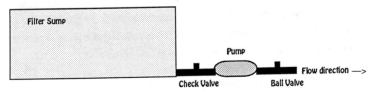

Depending on how elaborate your system is, or becomes, you may find it necessary to install more than one ball valve and more than one check valve. Refer to The Marine Fish and Invert Reef Aquarium, and also to Advanced Reef Keeping, for more details on how to set such systems up.

Some type of installations need 2 lines of water flow, e.g. one to the aquarium and one to the protein skimmer. This is done by means of a Tee-fitting, either barbed, or straight PVC. You may then need a second ball valve to adjust the amount of water going to the skimmer.

A typical installation, e.g. using the Thiel•Aqua•Tech filter, looks like this :

Only one ball valve is shown in the return line to the tank. That usually suffices, but as an extra safety, especially to make servicing of the pump itself easier, you may want to include an inexpensive ball valve (usually called throw away types) between the pump and the sump of the trickle filter. This will allow you to take the pump out of service without having to lower the water level in the sump.

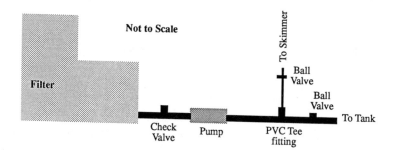

Although they will cost more money, "true union valves" are a much better choice than regular slip/slip valves. They are also easier to maintain, can be opened, and allow for easy and quick disconnection of pipes, should the need arise.

■ Adding Canister filters

Earlier I referred to installing extra compartments inside the sump of the filter. Not everyone wants to go to the trouble of doing so, or may not need to, because they have one or more canister filters standing around from previous filtration systems.

Canister filters obviously make great container/pump combinations for compounds through which the water needs to flow. I use them myself, and prefer the Eheim models 2217 and 2017 because of the large size of the canister itself. But there are, of course, other models available, for example Marineland's Magnum, and various Fluval types, including their large 403 model.

Since we are trying to set up a Reef Tank that will be correctly equipped on a smaller budget, you may want to shop around for canister filters. Try the bargain newspaper ad in your area. Or check if your Pet Store can sell you used ones.

Remember to change whatever compound you are using regularly. If, for instance, it is supposed to remove nitrates, as X-nitrate does, make sure that you test for nitrates from time to time, to double check whether your nitrates are still going down, or at least remain stable. If they do not, you obviously need to replace the compound. Using quick disconnect valves will make this a much simpler process.

■ Flow rates through Filters and the Tank :

First of all, you must differentiate between water flow through the system and water current in the tank. The former is pretty obvious: how much water is flowing through the filter, e.g. per hour. The latter represents the amount, and strength, of flow in the tank itself.

They are not necessarily the same. In fact they should'nt be. It is often recommended that you cycle the water content of your system anywhere from 2 to 6 times per hour through the filter. I find that latter figure much too high.

My recommendation in The Marine Fish and Invert Reef Aquarium was, and still is, that the water content of the tank be flowed through the biological filter 3 times per hour. More, and you risk bacterial wash-off, less, and you may not get enough biological filtration.

If you want more current in the tank itself, e.g. to simulate the wave action and movement around the Reef, use one or several power heads. One power head on the short side of the tank will usually do, but you can get more sophisticated, and use several that alternate, using an Ocean Motion machine, or similar. This was described in much more detail in Advanced Reef Keeping Made Simple.

The key to get the right flow rate, is to select your pump carefully. Ratings for pumps are given, most of the time anyway, at 0 feet of head, meaning when no back pressure whatsoever exists. This can mislead you, insomuch as you will be putting back pressure on the pump, and quite a bit of it, once you operate the tank . Here are just a few reasons for "head" (also called back pressure):
  ✳ height difference between the level of the pump itself (where it is positioned), and the water return level (how high up the water is being returned, meaning to the tank.

✳ the type of pipe or hose used. Is it of the same size as the output size of the pump, or are you downsizing

✳ are you downsizing the pipe or flexible hose elsewhere,

✳ is the intake pipe or hose the same as the pump fitting,

✳ are you using many fittings, especially 90° ells and 45° ells (angled fittings), as they reduce the flowrate greatly ,

✳ are you returning the water to the tank from the bottom, or from the top of the tank,

✳ is the pump pushing water through canisters, or other filters, that restrict the flow, especially once they start plugging up,

✳ are you using a micron, or submicron, filter in-line ?

Any and all of those, but usually a combination of them, added to frictional head, reduce the output of the pump, and result in the true output being quite somewhat lower than the stated output at zero feet of head. Frictional head is the head produced by the pipe or hose itself.

You should therefore think carefully before buying a pump. More so even when you plan to use the pump to run additional devices that require a good flowrate as well, and put additional back pressure (head) on the motor.

Talk to people in the Hobby that you respect, and who'se opinion you value and trust, e.g. a Pet Store owner or employee, someone at an Aquarium Society, a manufacturer, etc. Explain exactly what you are planning to do, then decide on which pump to buy.

Presently a lot of people use the Iwaki brand of pumps. I was responsible for introducing those pumps to the Hobby in 1987 on behalf of another company, and they had very good success with them. I have used many models myself, but have continued to look for a more aquarium specific pump, not one developed for the photographic chemical processing and similar industries.

This has led my company to putting together our own pumps, The Tech • Z series, labeled Za, Zb, Zc, Zd and Zz, putting out respectively 300, 600, 900, 1200 and 2400 gallons per hour. All these pumps have totally encapsulated impellers (polypropylene), use a special form of cooling and run very "cool" as a result, and incorporate only Viton seals. All these pumps carry a full one year warranty to boot.

Other brands you may wish to consider, US made ones, include Little Giant, March, Teel, and if you need a strong pump, Hayward. The latter only if you are using 1.5 or 2 inch pipe, and running a real large system. This is not something you would be doing on a small reef tank.

For medium type flow rates I strongly recommend the "Aqua Pump", a 3-speed model that is excellent for running the kind of tank that we are looking at in this book. It is super quiet, can be adjusted for output, and is made of a combination of 316SS and a plastic volute, totally salt water safe. This is definitely one of the pumps to consider for smaller systems.

It is also an excellent pump to run columnar skimmers with. I have used the Aqua Pump with 30", 46" and 84" skimmers, running the pump at respectively, 2nd, 2nd, and 3rd speed. In all cases it performed exactly the way I wanted it to and, combined with 2 airstones in the skimmers and a good air pump, it never let me down.

You must keep one important fact in mind when selecting a pump : the life of the animals and invertebrates that you want to keep, and for which you paid good money, depends on the pump that you ultimately select, running 24 hours a day, for many many years, hour after hour, day after day, month after month. Do not overlook this, invest in a good pump. Don't take any chances.

Pumps need to be cleaned from time to time, especially if its intake in the sump is not outfitted with a fine filter. Schedule it as part of your maintenance routine. Once every 3 months is probably a good timeframe. Additionally, open and clean the pump and impeller, any time you know for a fact that a large piece of dirt got into it.

Some general recommendations on installing and piping pumps:

➠ do not reduce the output side (pressure side) of the pump right at the pump. If you must reduce it, do so at least 18 inches away from the output fitting on the pump.

➠ never reduce the pipe going to the pump intake side (suction side). You will cause cavitation, and very small bubbles will always be visible in your tank because the water breaks up and the air comes out of it.

➻ buy a pump with at least 25-30 percent more rated output than what you feel you will need to run your tank. This will help offset the pressure head loss in output, and give a better flow.

➻ place the pump at the same level as the bottom of the sump. Not higher. Pumps sold for aquarium use do not "lift" water very well and you will strain the motor one one hand, and lose flow on the other, if you do. Additionally, it will be very difficult to prime the pump (get it started).

➻ often pumps can be used in only 1 or 2 positions. Check to make sure that the one you are using is an allowable one. (horizontal, upright, at an angle, sideways etc.)

➻ place pump on a thin piece of rubber, or foam, to reduce vibration and noise.

➻ clean your pump's volute and impeller at least once every 3 months.

➻ never let pumps run dry ! You will hear this often, but it is still done.

➻ if you pipe the pump using hose barbs and flexible tubing, use clamps as well, to prevent the hose from being blown off the barb, because of back pressure.

➻ preferably use a float switch to protect your pump.

➻ make sure no water falls or runs on the pump. If it does, clean up the water as soon as you can. Salt water is highly corrosive, and will ruin your pump in no time. Protect your investment, take good care of your pump.

■ Water Returns : One, Several, with or without bottom holes

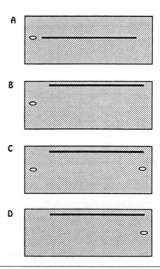

Water can be returned to the top or bottom of the tank, and you can use one or several water returns. How you set this up in your own tank will determine how you can populate the tank, as you do not want to cover up the water returns with rocks.

In smaller to medium size aquariums such as the ones discussed in this book, one water return is enough. Whether you return the water from the top, or whether you pipe it in through a hole in the bottom is entirely your decision.

● *Figures A   B   D* **(see previous page)**

Two water returns : the white hole is one, and the second one is through pipe, represented here by a thick black line. The entry point through the glass can be on the left, the right or the middle. In the former two cases you would use a 90° angled fitting coming out of the bulkhead (also called tank fitting), in the latter case you must use a Tee fitting, and capped-off pipe, going in either direction. The pipe in the middle, returns water underneath the rock formations and pushes the dirt out, so it can be filtered out or removed with a syphon hose, if you wish to do that.

D shows the same arrangement, but with the pipe placed towards the back of the tan and the hole on the other side. Which configuration you use is entirely up to you.

● *Figure C*

Three water returns : one on either side of the tank, and one underneath the rock formations to prevent water from stagnating there. The fittings used are described in A B D, above, and more details can be found in Advanced Reef Keeping I, also by Albert J. Thiel.

As already indicated, most Hobbyists will not need to drill holes in their tanks and can safely return the water from the top. Angle the jets downwards to stir up the bottom layers of water and bring them to the surface for better re-oxygenation.

Returning it from the bottom require more work, and the tank must be drilled. This is easy in an acrylic tank and somewhat more complicated in a glass tank. Some Pet stores now drill holes for you, or you can check with local glass dealers. As long as the bottom glass is not "tempered", drilling one or more holes is not really a problem.

The positioning of the return holes varies depending on whose recommendations you follow. Here are two possible suggested ways. I use the one with the two returns, one under the rock, and one at one end of the tank returning water from the bottom, against a side pane.

Sometimes spray bars are used to disperse the water over the water at the top of the tank. That may seem like a good idea, but it does not really create a great deal of water current and movement inside the tank. It should, therefore, in my opinion not be used in Reef Tanks.

■ Corner Overflows or Syphons-Surface Skimmers ?

To bring the water from the tank to the filter, Hobbyists use either corner overflow boxes or automatic syphon surface skimmers.

The use of corner overflows is rather widespread. Some tanks are sold with the overflow built-in, but more than likely, if you want to use that system, you will have to modify the tank.

Again, you will need a hole in the bottom of the tank (or the back, or the side, but obviously inside the overflow arrangement). You will have to build the overflow by using either 2 plates of glass, or 2 plates of acrylic to make a square or rectangular box (or one plate to make a triangular box, another possible arrangement that is not shown).

To affix the plates you will use aquarium silicone in glass tanks, and acrylic glue in acrylic tanks. Get plates of the same thickness as the aquarium glass or acrylic, using 3/8" as the maximum. This means that if your aquarium is made of 1/2" inch glass or acrylic, 3/8" will still do for the overflow. A 4" by 4" box is usually large enough for most tanks.

Because of the work involved, and the difficulty that you may have in your area to get glass drilled (acrylic is easy, and you can do so yourself with a good hole saw) many Hobbyists resort to the use of a syphon surface skimming arrangement.

There are quite a few on the market. Check around, and look for the following features :

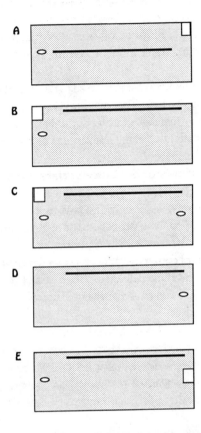

Various arrangements for corner overflows and returns
of the water through the bottom of the tank.

The black line represents a return behind and
underneath any coral and rock
formation you may have
placed in the tank.

There are, of course, still other possibilities.

♦ Can it handle the flow rate you are looking for ?

♦ Does it have a pre-filter built-in ?

♦ Can the pre-filter easily be removed and cleaned ?

♦ Is it glued properly, or do you see bubbles in the seams ?

♦ Is it easy to prime the first time you are using it ?

♦ Does it keep its prime, even if the pumps stop ?

♦ Will it fit over the ledge of your tank ? In glass aquariums such is usually not a problem, but in acrylic tanks with near complete tops, it often is.

♦ Will it skim the surface of the water in the tank and remove unwanted oily material, and floating particulate matter ?

These are all important considerations. Do not select a model too hastily. Look for at least most of the above features, especially the automatic re-starting one (meaning it keeps its prime even if the pumps stop). Having a pre-filter that can easily be serviced is also important.

Building your own is a consideration, but probably not worth the trouble. There is a large choice for you to select from, and in various price ranges. Buy only units that skim the surface properly, by means of a little box with indentations (tooth or comb-like) that hangs in the tank.

If you are planning to run more than 350 gallons per hour through the surface skimmer syphon, the one you buy should have a 1 inch hose adapter going to the filter. If it does'nt you may not be able to run your pump at the speed you want.

Of course, the unit you acquire should have a barb, or nip, in a convenient place (usually at the top), for you to be able to prime the syphon without much difficulty. The instructions should tell how to do so.

Clean the pre-filter at least once a week, lest it will start restricting the water flow down to the trickle filter, which will result in your pump stopping if you use a float switch, or running dry if you do not, and possibly failing, or running very hot.

Buy the right syphon-surface skimmer the first time around. You will save yourself both money and time, indeed, re-piping the system to replace the syphon is not something you want to look forward to.

If you decide to drill holes, to return the water to the tank, which in my opinion is not necessary in small and medium systems, make them at least 3/4 inch pipe size. This means the hole will have to be 1 inch, to accommodate the bulkhead-tank fitting.

■ Drip Systems as part of the Trickle Filter :

Although not something that you will find in too many filters, it is a nice and helpful addition. Use them to dispense liquid carbonate hardness (KH) generators, vitamins, Kalkwasser (Limestone water), even fertilizer if you keep a lot of macro-algae. In most cases, and because drip systems can only be regulated down so low, you will have to dilute whatever product you are adding before putting it in the drip system.

For more details on how to do so, and how to set up manual drip systems, we refer you to "Advanced Reef Keeping Made Simple" and also to "The Marine Fish and Invert Reef Aquarium" (6th or later printing), both by Albert J. Thiel.

■ Improving the Efficiency of your Existing Filter

Since many Hobbyists already own a trickle filter, we recieve many phone calls at "*Marine Reef*", the newsletter published by Aardvark Press, enquiring how one can improve the efficiency of an existing system. Since we are setting up a Reef Tank using only the minimum basic equipment required, it is most important that all the components of this system run at their optimum efficiency.

Here are a few suggestions :

▲ Blow more air into the biological chamber. Using regular aquarium air pumps, it is not possible to blow too much air in the chamber. Run the air through carbon first, to clean it.

▲ If you are not blowing air into it yet, start doing so, and make sure the drip plate is vented. Usually this is done by means of a piece of half inch, or three quarter inch, pipe sticking up from the drip plate. This will prevent an airlock from being created inside the biological chamber, should the water level in the sump rise to where the air can no longer escape through the bottom.

▲ If some of the media in the biological chamber is submersed, adjust the water level so it is out of the water. The efficiency of the filter will increase by over 50 percent. We guarantee it !

▲ Clean the sump of accumulated debris and detritus, this will increase dissolved oxygen levels and improve the water quality,

▲ Switch to a different medium inside the filter. For example, if you are using DLS, switch to one of the plastic filtering media. We highly recommend Bio•Techs and Bio Blocks. If you are using trays with dolomite or crushed coral, switch to a plastic filtering material as well. If you don't switch, clean the trays one at time, to remove accumulated detritus, at one week intervals, to prevent the total loss of the biological filtering bacteria.

▲ Switch from a "spray bar" filter to a "drip plate" filter type; better gaseous exhanges will take place, with the inherent improvement of the water chemistry,

▲ If you are already using a drip plate, improve its efficiency by using some, or all, of the recommendations we have made earlier. For example, increase the number of holes, but use smaller ones, and make the holes tapered.

▲ Add compartments for products such a Poly Filters, Chemi-Pure, X-nitrate, or whatever else you decide on using, including resins.

▲ Use one or more canister filters in addition to your trickle filter. Fill them with any of the above compounds, or use them for additional biological filtration by filling them with plastic filtering media. The efficeincy of Bio•Techs, used in submersed form, is 65 percent of their efficiency in non-submersed form. A large difference, but still quite of a lot of extra biological filtration ability.

▲ If you are using ozone, make sure none of it is finding its way into the back chamber (biological chamber) of your filter. Ozone will destroy some, or all, of the bacteria, and will greatly reduce the efficiency of your filter in the process.

▲ Set up a reverse osmosis drip system, running the output of the unit directly into your sump. Use a very small unit, and do not let it run continuously. Use it to change water very slowly, and make up for evaporation at the same time. If you let it run for long periods of time, the water level in the sump will rise, and could overflow, unless of course you have a drain piped in. This is done by running a hose attached to a tank fitting, placed at the appropriate height, from the sump to a drain, or to a sink that is lower than the sump (e.g. in a cellar).

If you do not have a drain, use a power head coupled to a float switch that kicks the pump on, when the level in the sump rises above a certain height. That water can then be pumped to a vat or sink, or wherever you can dispose of it. Always watch your salinity carefully when you are doing this, because you are adding fresh water, which will make your salinity go down slowly, but down nevertheless. Make up for this change in salinity, or specific gravity, at appropriate times.

▲ There are, I am sure, many other tried methods. If you have one that really worked for you, I would like to hear from you at Marine Reef, the Newsletter. We will compensate you for your contribution if it is published in the newsletter.

■ In-Line Cartridge Canisters :

These canisters, which can often be bought at do-it-yourself type hardware stores, and carry brand names such as Cuno, Water Kleen, AquaPure, etc. can be piped in-line with the water flow.

Some even have a by-pass assembly built-in to the unit, e.g. the units sold by Thiel•Aqua•Tech, making changing the cartridge very easy, because it does not require you to stop the system at all. Alternatively you can pipe-in the by-pass yourself.

Many types of cartdriges for such filters are available :
❑ to remove rust
❑ to remove fine particulate matter, rated in micron ratings
❑ filled with activated carbon
❑ filled with a mixture of compounds to purify the water

Keep in mind, when installing such in-line canisters, that they all put a lot of back pressure on your pump(s). This will reduce the water flow through the filters and through the tank.

Micron ratings go in various sequences, usually <1 micron, <1<5 micron, 5 micron, 25, 50 etc. microns. You should also know the difference between absolute and nomimal ratings. Absolute means no particles of the size given, or larger, can go through the cartridge. Nominal means "most" of the particle of the size given will get trapped, but some will get through. Nominal rated cartridges are good enough for our purposes, and 25 or 50 micron rated ones should take out most of the free floating material that you may want to remove. Do not go too low in the rating, because you do not want to filter out all of the living organisms, indeed filter feeders need them for survival.

Moreover, the finer filtering the cartridge performs, the sooner it will plug, and the sooner it will need replacing. That can add up to quite a few dollars, if you have to do so too frequently.

Two types of such cartridges deserve special mention, they are manufactured and sold by Poly-Bio-Marine (through their distributors) : the PMA and PSM types, the former performing molecular absorption filtration, and the second one sub-micronic filtration.

The one of most interest, in my opinion, is the PMA unit. They are specially tooled to be able to hold a number of disks, of Poly Filter material in disc form. Because of the way they are constructed, all the water has to go through the disks, before it can actually re-enter the main water stream.

Because Poly Filters are so highly efficient, and because these canisters are easy to install and service, we highly recommend them. In fact, I personally use them on all systems I install, and of course on my own show aquarium.

PSM canisters should not be used in continuous operation form in Reef tanks, because they remove all the material that filter feeders need. You should pipe them in so you can run them for a few hours, and then by-pass them without having to stop the system.

See the diagram on the next page for one method of piping in such a by-pass. The first canister shown could be any type, and is not required. It is shown here, because many Hobbyists use both PMA and PSM canisters in-line, one after the other. The first one should be the micronic, and the second one the molecular absorption one. The first one removes very fine particulate matter, and the second one acts as an extremely efficient chemical filter.

The water flow is from left to right.

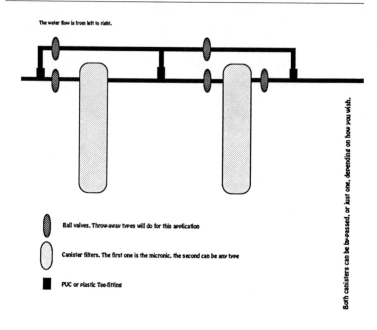

Ball valves. Throw-away types will do for this application

Canister filters. The first one is the micronic, the second can be any type

PVC or plastic Tee-fitting

Both canisters can be by-passed, or just one, depending on how you wish.

Remember to take the PSM cartridge off after you by-pass it, otherwise the water in the canisters will go anaerobic, and the next time you try to use it, you will push all that anaerobic material in the tank. Such is very dangerous for your invertebrates, and even for the fish you keep. With a properly set up by-pass, this problem does not arise. Just unscrew the bottom of the canister, rinse the bags inside, empty the canister and replace it.

The above diagram shows that you can isolate one or both canisters, meaning by-pass just the first one, or both, by switching the valves around. Under normal circumstances you would run the first canister, e.g. with a cartridge filter of, for instance, 25 or 50 microns, or a PSM module, and the second one with Poly Filters, X-nitrate, or some similar product.

Remember the remark about emptying the micron filter when it is not in use, to prevent the formation of anaerobic by-products. If you don't, the next time you place it back in line (use it) all these anaerobic compounds will end up in your sytem, and will create a great deal of stress on the tank life. It will greatly reduce your redox potential, reduce dissolved oxygen levels, and may even kill off some of the tank life.

■ Automatic Float Switches

We already covered float switches earlier. There is, however, one switch on the market that is both very reliable (over 100.000 operations) compact, and inexpensive that you may want to consider for your system : the Thiel•Aqua•Tech Super Float, which at the time of this writing retailed for $ 76.00.

It comes in a molded housing that you place into the sump, at the appropriate height, and connect into the pump wiring, as shown in the diagram. It can be used for inductive loads (e.g. pumps in our case) up to 5 amps, 110 volts. It should be affixed to the bottom of the sump, or vat, by means of a suction cup, or a little aquarium silicone. If it needs to be placed off the bottom, on a ledge of some sorts, because of the amount of water you keep in the sump, affix it to that ledge.

Note the following :

→ Only two wires come out off the Super float molded box. Some switches may have more wires, find out from the supplier which ones you should use to control the low, or high, triggering operation.

→ Only one of three wires that make up the pump lead that ends with a plug is used. Check the diagram carefully before wiring the switch in. The pump lead is the cord that comes off your pump.

→ This is called a splice, and where the commections are made, electrical tape has to be used to insulate the connections and make them water tight.

→ Never attempt to wire the Super float, or any other float switch while the pump is plugged in ! You will get an electrical shock.

→ Do not submerse the part of the electrical cord where you have made the splices, and covered them with electrical tape.

→ If you acquire the Super Float, do not operate it with pumps that draw more than 5 Amps. Check for the rating of other switches with whomever you bought it from. Operating a device at more than the rated amperage will ruin the device, in a short period of time, and can in some

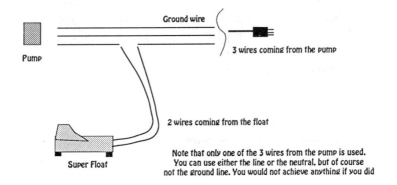

Note that only one of the 3 wires from the pump is used.
You can use either the line or the neutral, but of course
not the ground line. You would not achieve anything if you did

cases cause serious electrical shock.

→ The Super float, or any other float switch for that matter, must be placed in the sump, at the appropriate height. The installation of switches can sometimes be cumbersome, e.g. the orange german one available on the market. The Super Float is merely placed in the sump, on a base, if necessary, to adjust the height in deeper type sumps.

→ Incidentally, 100 000 minimum guaranteed operations of the switch, corresponds to about 5 years of continuous usage, with the switch going on and off about 55 times a day. That is most unlikely, on average, switches operate perhaps 10 to 15 times a day, if that much, greatly extending the guaranteed life of the switch.

→ Any pump can be operated with a float switch, including a power head type pump. Anything that works with electricity, in fact, can be operated with a float switch, providing , of course, that it makes sense to do so. Besides a pump, you may want to operate a solenoid that controls some outside device with such a switch. This is, however, not part of the basic system we are looking at in this book.

■ Converting from an Undergravel to a Reef System

While on the subject of biological filtration, let's review how one can convert a traditional undergravel system to a Reef Tank. Many Hobbyists, and you may be among them, already have a tank set up, either a fish-only, or perhaps even an aquarium with a mixture of fish and invertebrates, installed with undergravel plates, and perhaps one or several canister filters as well. Transforming such a system into a more modern one, using a trickle filter, is quite uncomplicated.

There are basically two major approaches :

❏ Maintain the undergravel system, while adding a trickle filter,

❏ Do away with the undergravel filter altogether.

You may elect to keep the canister filters, yet fill them with different compounds, e.g. chemical filters, as we shall see later.

Both are viable approaches, but the second one is the better one of the two, because it takes a potential area of low oxygen and pollution out of the system, while improving the overall quality of the biological filtration considerably. You may want to start with method one, let the tank run for a while in that fashion, and convert to a full Reef system at some later date.

➤ **Maintaining the Undergravel :**

→ Design the system you would like to end up with. Lay it out on paper, so you know what kind of parts and components you will need to acquire. Make sure all the parts will fit inside the aquarium cabinet. Measure carefully !

→ Obtain an appropriately sized trickle filter, taking the recommendations made earlier in this book into account.

→ Select an internal medium. Use one of the many plastic/polyethylene ones now offered for sale. Some Hobbyists use plastic hair-curlers. This may work, providing you use the clear ones that cannot leach a dye into the water. It would be safer however if you used a more traditional type of biological medium, e.g. Techs, Blocks, Spheres, Balls, Rings, Cubes, etc. There are plenty of them around.

→ Determine the quantity you need, based on the suggestions made in this, and other books.

→ Obtain a surface skimming syphon, preferably one that will re-start automatically, and keep its prime, even if the power and/or pump fails. This will make it unneccessary for you to re-prime it.

→ If you do not have one, buy a pump, and if you can budget for it, a float switch as well. It protects the pump and the system itself.

→ If you are not getting a protein skimmer right now, start thinking about it, because you will need it to maintain adequate water chemistry parameters. In light of this, you may want to get a filter with the right sized, ozone safe and resistent protein skimmer built-in.

→ Flexible vinyl, or acrylic, hose piping is an excellent way to go, and requires less time and expertise to install. Clamp all flexible hose connections to prevent slippage due to pressure, and leakage.

→ Install the filter and all other components of the system.

→ Do not forget to blow air into the biological chamber of your trickle filter. This is important for the potency (meaning how effectively it will perform) of your biological filter. Use a good, strong air pump. We suggest a Whisper 1000 or a pump with an equivalent output.

→ Fill the sump of the trickle filter with salt water, and start the pump, after priming the syphon of the surface skimmer.

→ Check all connections to ensure that you have no leaks. If you do, fix them now. Usually just tightening a clamp will do the job.

→ If need be, adjust the water level in the sump . Sometimes the pump will push up water so fast, that the sump water level becomes a little too low, and air gets sucked into the pump. If you have a float switch installed, the pump will shut off before that happens, providing you have set the float to kick on and off at the right level. If not, now is the time to adjust it, so it triggers at the correct level.

→ We have not mentionned the undergravel yet, because we do not want you to change anything to it, at least not yet.

→ Let the system run on both the undergravel, and the trickle filter, for one week to ten days. Because of the biological activity going on, and bacteria populating your new trickle filter, acidity is produced. This will affect both your carbonate hardness and the pH of the water. You should not worry about this, except if the pH goes down to dangerous levels e.g. 7.6 - 7.7. If this happens, you should add a carbonate hardness generator to your tank's water, preferably a liquid one, or a powdered, or tablet form, that does not make the protein skimmer foam excessively and starts overflowing.

→ Since your undergravel is still operating as it was before you added the trickle filter, water quality, as far as ammonia and nitrite are concerned, should not be a problem. In fact, if you had any before, you should'nt now. You have a better filter!

→ After 7 to 10 days you need to give your undergravel filter a serious cleaning. In order not to disturb the total undergravel biological filter, however, clean only 50 percent of the filter (e.g. one side of the tank, or just one plate if you have several).

→ After cleaning the undergravel filter, perform a 15 percent water change, and another 10 percent about 6 hours later.

→ now wait another 7 to 10 days, and clean the other half of the undergravel filter. Again, perform a 15 percent water change after the cleaning is completed, and a 10 percent water change approximately 6 hours later.

→ Next, reduce the flow of water going through the undergravel filter. *Do not stop the flow through the undergravel completely !* You would be creating an anaerobic environment very quickly if you did. Just slow the flow down to a minimum, much lower than what you had before. The reason for this, is that at a lower flow, detritus will not be pulled into the undergravel so easily, and no oxygen, or at least much less, will be taken out of the water by detritus breaking down in the undergravel filtration system. Your tank's water will, as a result, have a higher dissolved oxygen and redox potential level.

→ Check for ammonia and nitrite throughout the switch-over period. It is unlikely that any significant amounts will be found, although you may detect more of it than you normally would for a few days, especially right after you clean the undergravel filter.

→ Your switch-over is completed, and you now have a modern reef system. Clean your undergravel every 2 months or so, to remove detritus that may have accumulated.

➤ Converting and Removing the undergravel :

In the interest of maximizing water quality, it is much better, filtration-wize, when converting to a modern Reef System, to remove the undergravel filter completely. This may not be as practical as the previous solution, but it is definetely more effcient, and to the benefit of all tank lifeforms, especially the more sensitive corals and invertebrates.

Because of the nature of dolomite, or crushed coral, and the usual size in which it is sold as undergravel filter material, it easily traps detritus as water is pulled through it by the up-lift tubes and by, power heads. In fact more so with the latter.

Many Hobbyists will remark that reverse flow is a much better way of operating such filters, because the water can then easily be pre-filtered before it is pushed back through the filter bed itself, and into the aquarium. That is of course entirely correct, but detritus still gets trapped. It is just of a smaller size, and the clogging process will take longer to occur, but occur it will. Just stir up an old undergravel filter bed, and you will agree with me that the material that you can see coming out of the filter bed, cannot really be conducive to the higher water qualities that we are looking for in a Reef aquarium.

We are not saying that undergravel filters do not work, they do of course. If they did'nt, the hobby would not be where it is now. What we are saying is that you can do better, improve the water quality significantly, by removing the undergravel and switching over to a trickle filter as the sole biological filter of the tank.

The steps involved in doing this are similar to the ones described in the previous section, up to the point where we recommend that you clean half of the undergravel bed thoroughly. Instead of waiting 7 to 10 days, wait 14 days, meaning let both the undergravel and the trickle filter run the tank for 2 weeks, then remove half of the undergravel (or in larger tanks remove one third) **including the plates**.

This is labor intensive work for which you must plan, as it may take quite a while to do. After the plate, the crushed coral and dolomite are removed, perform a 20 percent water change. Wait about 6 hours, then perform another 10 percent water change. Since you may have two (or more) plates to remove this whole process may take up to 30 days to complete. Change plates at 10 day intervals, and perform water changes each time, as indicated.

The easiest way to remove the dolomite, or crushed coral, is to syphon it out with a large diameter hose. This will reduce the amount of material (detritus and mulm) getting into the water. You will be removing water at the same time, which you need to do anyway, because of the recommended water changes. Watch the pH, and add a carbonate hardness generating fluid (or tablets, powders without binders), if it drops too low. Beware of products that contain nothing else but baking soda !

➻ Remarks on the Conversion Process :

❑ Because in both types of conversions the existing undergravel, and the new trickle filter, are running at the same time, the seeding of the new filter with bacteria is automatic, and the cycling happens without the Hobbyist noticing it. Indeed, you already had a lot of bacteria in the system. They are being transferred to a different medium.

❑ As long as the existing undergravel filter was able to keep ammonia and nitrite down to zero, no increase will be noticed in the first 7-14 days, while both filters are running together.

❑ After cleaning the undergravel (in one scenario) and removing part of it (in the other), a small amount of ammonia and nitrite may be present for a few days. The amount will, however, not be high and stress on the fish will be minimal. There will be some degree of stress that the animals will have to cope with, that is unavoidable, indeed, you **are** making changes.

❑ Do not add any fish or invertebrates whatsoever during the conversion process! None whatsoever.

❑ Clean all mechanical filters before you start the conversion.

❑ To alleviate stress on the tank life change your Poly Filters if you are using them already. If you are not, we suggest that you add 1 Filter per 25 gallons of water in the system. To find that number, add the volume of water that is in the sump, to the gallon content of the tank. Multiply that by 90 percent (to account for displacement by rocks etc..) and use that number.

❑ Remember that the water going to the trickle filter needs to be pre-filtered. If you don't do so, you will have to clean the drip plate of the filter regularly. Good quality syphon surface skimmers will have such a pre-filter built-in.

❑ If you are using a spray bar, which we recommended you did'nt, pre-filtering is even more important.

❑ The recommended water changes that go in hand with the cleaning of the undergravel filter, and removing the plates, are very important. They are meant to remove the noxious toxins that result from stirring up the material used on the filter plates, from the water. Not doing so may lead to a lot of problems.

❑ In the first type of conversion, where the undergravel filter is not removed, you must clean the undergravel filtering medium very thoroughly, to remove any material that can cause oxygen depletion, anaerobic activity, plugging of the crushed coral or dolomite, etc.

❑ In the second type of conversion, where the undergravel is removed in several stages (at least two), it is very important that the medium on the filter plates be **syphoned** out. This will prevent the detritus in the crushed coral, or dolomite, from mixing with the tank's water. Some of it will, but you must try to minimize that mixing as much as possible, because of the toxins it also contains.

❏   Remember not to turn the undergravel filtering system pumps (air or power heads) completely off. Reduce the throughput, but do not shut it off completely. If you do, the layer of water underneath the plates, and the material on the plates, will quickly produce anaerobic by-products. This may kill off everything you keep in the tank. Many Hobbyists have made that mistake before you, and have wondered why, even though they added a trickle filter, they could not raise the water quality.

❏   Do not rush the conversion. Take your time. Follow the suggested timeframe. Your fish and invertebrates will benefit from it.

❏   If you were using canister filters in conjunction with your undergravel filter, you can certainly continue to use them with the new filtration you installed. It seems, however, that they should then be used for other purposes : additional mechanical filtration (clean them at least once a week), chemical filtration (see next section), special compounds e.g. to remove nitrate from the water, etc.Run them, taking water from the sump, and returning it to the sump.

❏   Because of the changes you are making to the filtration, initially, changes to the water chemistry will affect the redox potential; it will go down, but come back up after a few days, to a week maximum.

❏   Dissolved oxygen and carbon dioxide levels will also be affected, but not to the point where you have to be concerned about it.

Changing over to trickle filtration is a positive move. It will take time to perform, but it will greatly benefit your system in the short, and long run. It definitely is a positive step for the water quality, and ultimately for how your tank will look some weeks down the road.

■ Chemical Filtration

■ General Remarks

This is probably the least understood form of filtration that is required in fish-only as well as in Reef tanks, even more so in the latter.

Mechanical filtration removes particulate matter of varying sizes; biological filtration removes ammonia and nitrite by means of bacterial processes, and converts it to nitrate; chemical filtration removes yet other types of compounds, some of which are not normally removed by the former, some of which are to not removed by protein skimmers either (see next section).

The best known form of chemical filtration is activated carbon, others include molecular absorption filters (e.g. Poly filters), resins (e.g. HyperSorb), and special compounds meant to selectively remove certain elements from the water.

What kind of compounds are we talking about ? Besides the undesirable elements already mentioned, e.g. free floating material, nitrogen breakdown intermediates, seawater absorbs many noxious elements from the surrounding air (e.g. nicotine, tar, fumes, perfume essence, volatile organic compounds etc..), chemicals that, when they accumulate, can stress the tank life considerably.

Besides these, many chemical compounds are formed in the

aquarium and are not removed by the filters already mentioned. Included in this category are, for example, yellowing matter (gilvin), organic acids, heavy metals that may come in with the tap water, pesticides in very small quantities (ppb's), etc.

The principles of chemical filtration are based on molecule adsorption, and on ion affinity, allowing certain compounds that we add to the filtration system to remove unwanted elements very efficiently. Because we do not "see" the filter at work, certainly not as much as we can determine what a mechanical filter is doing for example, these type of filters can be extremely beneficial, especially if the material used is replaced on a regular basis.

I conducted many experiments along the lines of chemical filtration, using an assortment of chemical filtering materials. All work, some **much** better than others. Two types in particular are very familiar to most hobbyists : activated carbon and Poly Filters. Resins and other compounds are used less frequently, except perhaps for the "X-nitrate" compound from Thiel•Aqua•Tech, which is very specific for Nitrate ions, and can lower the total NO_3 in seawater to the 2-5 ppm range in a matter of 7 to 10 days. Unlike carbon, this product cannot be regenerated. Then again, regenerating carbon is not recommended anyway, as Hobbyists do not really have the equipment to do so efficiently.

■ Activated Carbon

Many types of carbon are sold in Pet Stores. Unfortunately the Hobbyist has no way of knowing which ones are good, bad or better. Some brands are merely charcoal (usually shiny) and are very ineffective at removing noxious compounds. You should definitely avoid them in Reef Aquariums.

Other types are "activated", a process that substantially increases the porosity of the carbon, and as a result greatly increases the total active surface area, usually depicted in drawings as an intricate path of holes, and channels, in the carbon, allowing it to be much more eff-ective at adsorbing compounds that need to be removed from the Reef tank's water. The amount of pores and channels is what is of interest to us.

Activated carbon has a maximum adsorption capacity, which is the reason that it should be replaced from time to time. How frequently is hard to determine, because it is dependent on the quality of the water that is flowed through the carbon. Note that we said flowed "through" and not over. Your activated carbon will work much better if water is actually forced to go through the amount used, rather than just flowed by, and over it. More contact between the activated carbon and the water obviously results in a more efficient cleansing process.

One problem that frequently occurs in saltwater tanks with a heavy organic load, is that the outside of the carbon becomes quickly coated with organic matter and slime, preventing further uptake and adsorption of unwanted compounds from the water.

How much carbon you should use, if you decide on this method of chemical filtration, is open to much debate. Some advocate small quantities of only a few ounces per 50 gallons of water in the system, to quantities that are 7 to 8 times larger.

Our recommendation is that if you use a good quality brand, you can safely follow the manufacturers' recommendations. Perhaps the most frequently recommended type is Chemi Pure from Dick Boyd Enterprises. It has been around for along time, and has obviously proven itself to many Hobbyists. We use our own Tech•Coconut•Shell brand.

Activated carbon is used to remove DOC (dissolved organic compounds), yellowing matter, heavy metals e.g. copper and iron (to some extent), airborne pollution, trace elements, intermediate protein breakdown products, and so on. Quite an amount of elements indeed. It is, therefore, an efficient chemical filtration material.

Since it removes trace elements as well, it is important to perform water changes from time to time (4 to 5 percent a week is my usual recommendation) to replenish such needed elements, or add one of the commercially available trace element mixes (e.g. Reef Elements from T•A•T, CoraLife, HW Trace Elements, Tropic Marine, etc.)

When using activated carbon, keep the following in mind :
❑ Smaller granules, or pellets, will do a much better job,

because of a higher total surface area, meaning greater porosity.

❑ If only small amounts of activated carbon are used, you will need to replace it often, perhaps as much as every 2 to 3 weeks.

❑ Rinse all activated carbon before using it, to remove fine material and dust, that will otherwise end up in the tank and on the rocks. This black dust is hard to remove, and makes the tank look very unsightly, besides being noxious to fish and invertebrates.

❑ Ensure that a good "through" flow takes place. Do so by placing the carbon in a compartment of the trickle filter through which all the water **has** to flow, or better still :

❑ place the activated carbon between layers of polyester floss filtering material, in a good quality canister filter. The new Eheim 2200 series canisters are highly recommended as they offer good flow and move quite a bit of water. Magnum and Fluval are other choices.

❑ Because good quality activated carbon is expensive, it is important to pre-filter the water that goes through the canister or the compartment in the filter, to prevent the carbon from becoming coated with fine particulate matter, and acting as a mechanical rather than chemical filter. This ruins the efficiency of the activated carbon fast.

❑ Test the carbon that you plan to use for leaching of phosphate. Soak some carbon in a little tap water, or aquarium water, wait about 6 hours. Now take a sample of the water and test it for phosphate content. You will be surprised to find the number of brands that actually leach phosphate into the aquarium. Such types of activated carbon are of course totally unacceptable for use in Reef Aquariums. J. Asero (1989) evaluated many types of carbon, and found only few that did not leach carbon in the water. For a more detailed review we refer you to Marine Reef, the newsletter, Volume 2 Number 20.

❑ Some carbons may also leach sulfate, and metals, into your water. Make sure you buy top quality carbon and you will avoid these problems. Coconut shell carbon is probably the best, but also the most expensive. In a Small Reef you should not take any chances.

❑ Make sure that you change the activated carbon regularly. Many types of carbon are known to leach some of the matter they first adsorb back into the water, once they have exhausted their ability to remove matter from the water. Chemically speaking what may be at work here, is ion displacement , with the ones for which the carbon has more affinity displacing ions for which there exists lesser affinity. The displacement results in these ions ending back up in the water (Thiel, 1989).

❑ Exhausted activated carbon will soon start acting as a small biological filter and will also, as time goes by, act as a mechanical filter. This is not desirable because you have no control over what compounds leach back into the water. Spent activated carbon should, therefore, be removed and replaced. You can tell whether your carbon is still "working" (removing compounds from the water) by checking whether your water is yellowing. Make a very faint yellow mark on a small piece of white plastic, submerse it and look at it from about 12 to 18 inches away. If you cannot see the difference between the very faint yellow and the white, your water is obviously slightly yellow, and your carbon needs changing.

❑ Some lesser quality types of activated carbon may alter the pH too much. Usually they will raise it. Sometimes considerably. Acid washed carbon will not.

❑ Fresh activated carbon will lower dissolved oxygen levels for a short period of time, and may as a result lower your redox potential as well. This is however short lived.

❑ Soak new carbon in warm water to remove gas bubbles trapped in the pores. This will improve the efficiency of the carbon substantially.

❑ When in doubt about the freshness of your carbon, do not use it, or if it is in your filter already, change it.

❑ You may also want to filter the air going into your trickle filter by running it through a small column of carbon first. This will remove airborne pollutants. An old air dryer that you are not using can be filled with a good brand of carbon and place in-line with the air flow. Some units are commercially available (e.g. T•A•T).

❑ Carbon removes organics from the water, to some extent anyway, but does not do away with the need to use a properly sized protein skimmer on your system as well. All you get is some degree of polishing of the water, not total removal. Refer to the section on protein skimmers for more details.

❑ Pulverized activated carbon offers the largest surface area of all carbons. It is however not as easy to use, and needs to be set up with a diatom filter, or low micron filter, at the same time. This will result in the need to change the carbon frequently, as diatom and low micron cartridges, or special very low mesh bags, will of course plug up faster, as they trap very small particulate matter as well.

❑ Of all the activated carbon types I have used myself, I prefer a granule, about one eight to three sixteenths of an inch in diameter. The granules must be "dull", not shiny ! Of course, that is the kind my company sells, as it is the one that I have found works best.

❏ Do not overlook the need to add carbon to the system if you are using ozone. Best is to flow the water coming out of the skimmer over a little activated carbon, before it can re-enter the main water stream back to the aquarium. Trickle filters that have compartments built-in that allow you to do so are, therefore, to be preferred.

❏ Although at some time I was convinced, based on experiments, that in the case of activated carbon "more was better", I have since changed my recommendations. I now recommend approximately one half pound of activated carbon of very high quality per 75 gallons of water, with the stipulation that the activated carbon must be changed every 5 weeks, regardless of how well the tank may be doing. This will ensure that the carbon is always removing pollutants from the tank.

❏ You can safely mix several forms of chemical filtration. For example, you can use activated carbon and resins, or activated carbon and molecular absorption pads (Poly Filters) or disks (PMA discs from Poly-Bio Marine) . The latter of the two is the better.

It may appear to you, that selecting carbon has become a little more complicated than it used to be. Indeed it is. Unfortunately the better qualities we refer to are hard to come by. Knowing all the problems associated with activated carbon, my own company obviously sells only top quality coconut shell, acid washed to ensure a stable pH.

■ **Deionizing Resins :**

Before deciding to invest in a D.I. unit, read this section several times, especially the parts dealing with regenerating the resins. The latter is not simple, and can be dangerous.

Even though I have looked for resins that perform consistently well in a salt water environment, I have not yet been able to find such a resin. What I am looking for is a resin that is a very specific though.

Some resins can, of course, be used, but they exhaust their adsorption ability very quickly and are, therefore, in my mind, a waste of money. What happens is that the exterior of the resin becomes coated with larger ions (e.g. sodium and chloride) and a protein surface coating from the organic load of the water. As a result no other ions can migrate to the inner structure of the resin, where the larger part of the adsorption takes place. This, then, results in a very very poor utilization of an expensive medium.

If you are trying to remove nitrates, phosphates, and heavy metals from the tank itself, disregard using deionizing resins until such time as much more efficient types become available. Beware, of anyone trying to sell you a resin that will do all sorts of wonders for your tank. So far I have not found one, but some will appear, hopefully soon.

Resins should be used to treat the water to which you will be adding salt, before you actually add the salt, to remove impurities, nitrates, phosphates, and so on. Such treated water can then be safely added to the tank. In some cases it will be necessary to aerate the water before using it, because the de-ionized water will be very low in dissolved oxygen. It is a good idea to test for D.O. the first time you use whatever resin you may have acquired. This will tell you whether to expect low D.O. in the effluent water or not, allowing you to determine whether or not to aerate it first.

Many resins that will "purify" tap and well water are available. The key is to get the kind that will do exactly what you are looking for, can be easily recharged, or regenerated, using chemicals that can easily be obtained, and can be used without undue precautions.

There are basically 2 types of resins available to the Hobbyist:
→ Anion resins (pronounced an__ion)
→ Cation resins (pronounced cat__ion)

Resins are sold as monobed (one resin) or mixes (e.g. 2 resins). To confuse you a little, the word monobed is sometimes used to refer to a single deionizing column (device), that may contain a mixture of 2 resins (monobed = 1 bed of resins).

In double columns, the ones where 2 resins are used, and are kept separated, the cation exchange resin must be used first. The water flows first through the cation column and then from the cation resin to the anion resin. Flow rates recommended vary greatly; the best results are usually obtained with flow rates of 1-2 gallons of water per minute, per cubic foot of resin. Since most Hobbyists' deionizers only contain about 1/6 of a cubic foot, the flow rates should be adjusted accordingly to about 10 to 20 gallons per hour. If your unit contains even less, e.g. only 1/8 of a cubic foot, the recommended flow rate is 7 GPH. Very slow indeed.

Although recirculating the water through the resin will work, most manufacturers recommend "single pass" operations. This means that the water to be treated is flowed only once through the resin, and as slowly as possible. This is also what I now recommend you do.

Slow flow rates, such as the ones mentioned, are best obtained by gravity feed, without the use of a pump. Just let the water flow slowly through the resin. In two column units, first through the cation and then through the anion. In single mixed bed resin units the principle is the same, let the water flow slowly from the top of the column to the bottom, in a single pass treatment fashion.

The useful life of resins is theoretically indefinite, because, once exhausted, the resins can be recharged, regenerated, and used again as new. Practically, this is however not the case. Some resin will be lost, e.g. when regenerating, and you will need to add resin to the unit at some point. Not a lot, but you may find that after several months (6-7) you may need to add a pound or so.

Hobbyists never have a problem installing a de-ionizing unit. Problems come about when regeneration time comes around. Here are two ways to approach this matter, depending on whether you are using a single or double column unit (remember : regenerating resins can be dangerous if you are not familiar with the use of the chemicals needed):

◆ Double de-ionizing Units :

These units consist of two columns, one filled with a cation exchanger and one filled with an anion exchanger resin. Each of the columns requires a different recharging method.

Cation Resin Exchanger :

Prepare a solution of 4 percent acid content. For every pound of resin you have, you will need about 2 gallons of water to treat the resin (water that has been treated with acid). To make a 4 percent acid solution you will need HCl or H_2SO_4, not something you usually have standing around, unless you are a chemist, a doctor, etc..

Swimming Pool places, and some hardware stores, sell a product called "Muriatic acid". This is usually a 32 percent or a 20 percent solution of HCl (hydrochloric acid). It will say so on the bottle. Muriatic acid can be further diluted to obtain a 4 percent HCl solution, that you can then run slowly through your de-ionizing cation exchange resin. Lower HCl solutions, e.g. 10 % are sold too. They should be preferred as they are less dangerous to use.

Remember to use great caution when working with Muriatic acid. Acids can burn your skin, damage clothing, furniture, carpets etc... Read the instructions very carefully, and if you are not sure about what to do, don't do anything. Ask someone who knows. If you spill any on yourself, you must wash it off immediately. **Never add water to the concentrated acid. You must add acid to water and very slowly. Stay away from sulfuric acid, it is a much more dangerous acid chemical.**

For example : you buy a 32 percent HCl Muriatic acid. The bottle holds half a gallon. If you now add this half gallon of Muriatic acid very slowly to half a gallon of water, you have a 16 percent solution, and a total of one gallon of water. Adding this to a gallon of water will give you a total of 2 gallons, and an 8 percent solution. Adding this to another 2 gallons of water will give you a total of 4 gallons and a 4 percent solution of HCl. Remember HCl is a very acid chemical and can easily burn your skin, carpets, clothes, furniture....Use care and good judgement, and keep all chemicals away from children.

Four gallons is enough to treat 2 pounds of resin. If you have more resin, you will need to make more 4 percent solution. If you had, for instance, 5 pounds of resin, you will need to make 2.5 times the above quantity.

Another example : You buy a one gallon bottle of 20 percent HCl solution Muriatic acid. Add this to one gallon of water and you have a 10 percent solution and 2 gallons total. Add this to 2 gallons of water and you have 4 gallons total of a 5 percent solution. To go from a 5 % solution to a 4 %, you need to reduce the concentration by 20 % because 80 % of 5 = 4.

This may seem complicated at first, but it is'nt really. Granted, you may have to do some calculations, but as long as you know the concentration of the muriatic acid, you should not find it difficult to get to the right dilution quickly.

Remember that you are working with an acid, and that you should follow the precautionary instructions that come with the Muriatic Acid you bought. Especially, keep it away from children. If you do not know how to work with such chemicals stay away from them. Use a different method to purify the water. We highly recommend molecular absorbtion (see the section on water purification).

Once you have prepared the necessary quantity of treatment water, run it through your de-ionizer slowly, 0.5 gallons per minute is plenty (± 30 gallons per hour). Collect the outflowing water/acid mix, and dispose of it safely. Do not store it. Get rid of it safely right away. You cannot use it a second time ! Best is to add it to a bucket full or two of more water to dilute it even further.

After you have treated the resin, you must flush it with distilled, or previoulsy deionized, water to remove the acid form the column. If you don't do this, the first couple of gallons coming out of the unit will be very acid, and will not be useable unless you first neutralize the acidity with e.g. Calcium or Sodium carbonates or bicarbonates. Flushing is usually much easier and is, therefore, to be recommended.

Anion Exchange Resin :

Anion exchange resins must be regenerated separately from the cation resins, and this time using a 4 percent base solution (with a high pH).

You must now prepare a 4 percent solution based on the method already described, using Sodium Hydroxide. This can usually be obtained from hardware stores as caustic soda, as it is also used to unclog clogged drain pipes of sinks.

Because this is a stronger chemical, please follow the directions on the can or bottle or container very carefully. You are not doing anything dangerous, but you must be careful, that's all. Keep the mixture and the chemicals away from children. Dispose of the effluent safely by diluting it even further.

Run the mixture slowly through the resin, again at about 30 gallons per hour, and this time use 3 gallons per pound of resin you have. Dispose of the effluent safely and immediately. Do not store it. You can not re-use it. Flush the unit slowly to remove all remaining caustic material, lest the pH of the water you will treat will be too high.

When should you regenerate ?

• when the resin is no longer removing all the elements you want to remove, e.g. nitrates and phosphates.
• when total dissolved solids measure more than 30-40 ppm. Small, inexpensive, handheld units measuring TDS are advertised in hobby magazines, or can be bought from scientific supply houses.

◆ Single de-ionizing Units :

Single column de-ionizers, using a mixed bed (2 resins), are regenerated in exactly the same manner as double units, but first the resins need to be separated.

First you must remove the resin from the container. Place it in a larger one, at the bottom of which you have placed one or two air stones. Place filter floss over the resin, as well as a rather tight fitting lid with some holes in it, for the water to come through.

Now pump water slowly into that vat, from the bottom, and blow air slowly as well at the same time. The action of the water and of the air will make the lighter anion resin migrate to the top, and the heavier cation exchanger will go to the bottom. In the middle a small band of mixed resin will remain. Old columnar protein skimmers make ideal containers to do this, as long as you pump the water in through the original "outflow" of the skimmer, and let the water come out where it would normally have gone in when the unit is run as a skimmer (you are in essence reversing the in and out).

Remove the anion resin and treat as indicated in the previous section. Remove the mixed resin layer and dispose of it. It cannot be separated easily, and can not be recharged. Since mixed bed exchangers contain equal amounts of both types of resin, the mixed layer is in the middle. Remove the cation exchange resin, and treat as explained in the previous section.

General Remarks on Resins :

❑ Never deionize water to which salt has been added already.

❑ The better the water you start with, the longer your resin will obviously last.

❑ Some Hobbyist first use reverse osmosis, then deionize.

❑ Regenerate frequently. The effluent water will always be better.

❑ In double units always run water through the Cation resin first.

❑ Flowing water through activated carbon before D.I. extends the resin life.

❑ Flowing water through carbon after D.I. "may" purify the water more and better. It is better to put it before the D.I. unit.

❑ Flowing water thru Poly Filters after D.I. will purify the water even more.

❑ Flowing water thru Poly Filters before D.I. will extend the resin life.

❑ Remove all water from D.I. units that are not in use, and/ or stored.

❑ Turn units not in use upside down in a bucket or so.

❑ If water remains in a unit when not in use, it will stagnate and smell because of anaerobics.

❑ Before each session of D.I. flush the unit with some water.

❑ If the outcoming water smells at first, flush it until it does'nt anymore. Or regenerate the resins.

❑ Check the D.O. of the outflowing water periodically. If need be, aerate the water to re-increase the dissolved oxygen.

❑ Be very careful with the regenerating compounds.

❑ Keep them away from children.

❑ After regenerating, dispose of effluent safely and immediately. See the main text for methods of how to do so.

❑ Always rinse resin well after regenerating to remove acids and bases, lest the pH will be too low or too high for the water to be used.

■ Molecular Absorption Filters :

Of all the chemical filtration methods available to the Small Reef Hobbyist, perhaps the easiest to use, and certainly the easiest to install and include in the filtration set-up, is the very well-known Poly Filter from Poly-Bio Marine.

A pad, or disks, are placed anywhere in the water flow, as long as they are in an area where water flows "through" them. They will work too if water just flows "by or over" them, but they will give you their full efficiency if water flows "through" them.

Poly Filters are a synthetic material impregnated with hydrophylic polymers designed to remove pollutants from the water by absorbing their molecules.

Some of the compounds these pads or discs will remove, or reduce, or keep in check, include the following :

→ phosphates : mineralized or ortho-phosphate,
→ copper : chelated and non-chelated
→ ammonia, ammonium ion
→ airborne pollutants from fumes, sprays, etc..
→ organic breakdown pollutants,
→ medicine,
→ amines
→ uric acid
→ tannins, phenols, humic acid

→ volatile organic compounds (VOC's))
→ organic phosphate

The pads, or discs, can be placed anywhere in the water flow. Moreover, not all of them have to be in the same spot. You can distribute them in several locations, wherever you have space, and wherever the water will flow through them. Additionally, feel free to cut them up in smaller pieces of any shape, and make them fit the space where you have decided to place them.

They change color as they become progressively loaded with the compounds they have removed, they start to change color. This allows you to determine when, in fact, it is time to replace them. Because they may also trap dirt, their true color may be masked. It is, therefore, a good idea to clean them once a week to remove particulate matter that they may have trapped. Rinse them under warm tap water and squeeze to remove dirt. Evaluate the color after you have cleaned the pads or discs. If they start to turn medium to dark brownish, it is time to replace them.

Here are some typical colors the pads or discs may take on, and the products that are involved. This list was provided by Ken Howery of Poly-Bio Marine Inc. :
- Blue   : copper salts
- Blue/greenish : copper ion
- Greenish/ yellow : ammonia, amines
- Orange : iron
- Red : aluminum used in water treatment
- Brown : normal organic load
- Black : heavy organic load, high protein waste
- Yellow : Ethyl Lead

I have personally used, and still use, Poly Filters for years. I would not run a tank without them. This is a truly superior product that you **must** include in your filtration set-up. I use a lot of them. Sometimes one pad per 25 gallons of water. If there was such a thing as a Reef Tank Best Product Award, Poly Filters should get it. Poly Filters are widely available and, because of their relatively long life, are a very cost efficient chemical filter.

The pads, when new, are white. Do not buy pads that have a faded yellow color. They may be old, and although they will still work, they will exhaust themselves rather quickly. Make sure the package is closed when you get it.

Some locations where you could place a Poly Filter :
- in the sump, close by the pump intake opening,
- in the sump in a special compartment that is already there, or that you have added,
- in the pre-filter box, or overflow syphon arrangement,
- in a canister filter,
- in a chemical module of e.g. Lifeguard or PEP filters,
- in the overflow corner box, if your tank was drilled for one,
- inside the tank in an inconspicuous area with good water flow, for example behind rocks, or dead coral,
- and of course in the special canisters sold by Poly-Bio Marine.

Some Hobbyists dedicate a Poly Filter to remove copper from hospital or treatment tanks, and use that pad only for that purpose. Such is, of course, an excellent idea. So is having such a small tank running at all times. Just in case !

If you use Poly Filters to remove medications, use one pad per type of medication and remove it after the treatment is completed. Store the pad after letting it dry, and label it so you know what medication you used it for. Poly Filters do not remove gasses, so they will not affect your dissolved oxygen and carbon dioxide levels. That is a boon, because freshly added carbon will, for some time, lower the D.O. levels. The latter, in turn, affects your redox potential.

Keep a few spare pads around. When something just does not seem right with the tank (and such happens, believe me), add one or more Poly Filters immediately. Of course you must, in such cases, also check your water quality parameters, and make adjustments if necessary. Sometimes, however, things seem not right, and no cause can clearly be identified. As a precaution and partial or complete remedial, Poly Filters should be added to the system.

I indicated already that Poly Filters should be cleaned. Because even in the best filtered tanks small particulate matter always abounds, it is necessary to do so regularly. Make it part of your regular mainte-nance routine. Your water quality will benefit from it. And, when keeping Reef Tanks, it all boils down to water quality.

When placing Poly Filters in a canister filter, position them between layers of filter floss. This will reduce the amount of particulate matter trapped on the pads or disks, and make them perform more effi-ciently for you.

As far as I have been able to determine, Poly Filters will not remove ozone, and Poly-Bio Marine are looking into this. However, a Poly filter that has been in use for a while will reduce it, mainly because of the particulate matter it has trapped. Some carbon is, therefore, still necessary if you run a skimmer, or a reactor, with ozone injection.

We referred to pads and discs in this section. Although they both perform the same function, the discs are a much stronger variety of the medium. The latter also explains why they are more expensive.

■ Additional Remarks on the Use of Activated Carbon :

Earlier in this chapter we looked at the uses of activated carbon. My intentions were not that say that activated carbon is not an efficient chemical filter. It certainly is. The point, however, is that in Reef and Marine tanks you can do better, for example by using Poly Filters or molecualr absorption discs.

Keep in mind also that there are many varieties of activated carbon offered for sale, to name a few :
  → coal based, mixed types
  → bituminous
  → lignite
  → coconut shell
  → vegetable base (other than coconut)

The better types of activated carbon are definitely lignite and coconut shell, the latter being the best one for our application. If it is not acid washed first, and then rinsed, both done during the manufacturing process, the effluent water's pH will be too high. If you decide to use that type, make sure such was done, so the pH of your Reef does not get affected (as already indicated, usually upwards).

I personally prefer the small granules described earlier. These seem to give the best wetting of all the carbon. The latter means that all granules are exposed to the water that flows through the activated carbon, which is, of course, what we must try to achieve, as such ensures better adsorption, and cleansing of the water.

■ **Review of Filtration Requirements Discussed:**

→ **Mechanical Filters :**
→ Use one or more mechanical filters and clean them frequently.
→ They can be before the trickle filter, and/or in the sump.
→ Use a canister filter if an extra mechanical filter is necessary.
→ Make sure they can be easily accessed.
→ Don't use diatomaceous earth filters.
→ Sub-micron filters should only be used intermittently.
→ Filter floss is perhaps the most economical way to go.
→ Repeat : clean filters regularly. Once a week is a minimum

→ **Biological Filters**
→ Use an under the tank trickle filter or hang-on trickle filter.
→ Select one that has most of the desirable features mentioned earlier in the book.
→ Make sure that it has a large sump area.
→ Strong aeration of the biologial chamber is a must.
→ Fill it with plastic filtering media, e.g. balls or blocks.
→ If it has a built-in skimmer, it should be of the right size.
→ We prefer drip plates with tapered holes, over spray bars.
→ 1/4 inch thick acrylic material is recommended.
→ Do not run too much water thru the biological chamber.
→ Pre-filter the water that enters the biological chamber.
→ Do not use plastic media that trap dirt.
→ Repeat : blow lots of air in the biological chamber.
→ Open up plugged holes in the drip plate if you see any.
→ Syphons with a surface skimmer are better.

→ syphons with an automatic re-start are better.

→ Use a properly sized pump AND a float switch.

→ **Chemical Filters :**

→ Use molecular absorption filters liberally.

→ We highly recommend Poly Filters pads or discs.

→ You must use some carbon as well, if you inject ozone.

→ You can use both activated carbon and Poly Filters.

→ We prefer small granules, about 4 mesh size.

→ Change your activated carbon frequently.

→ Make sure it does not leach phosphates in your water.

→ It. should have been acid washed to prevent a pH rise.

→ If you plan to use resins, read the earlier section a few times.

Remember, now is the time to make the right decisions. Before you buy the equipment. Spend once, and acquire the right product the first time around. Remember too, that most of the above features can be combined in one and just one correctly selected trickle filter. Canister filters, where recommended, are optional, yet very desirable.

Foam Fractionators - Protein Skimmers

Yet another most controversial piece of equipment, although its use has greatly increased in the last few years, thanks to several articles on the subject in Hobby magazines. **My own position is very clear : they are necessary, they are here to stay, they must be carefully sized, and you may have to use ozone with them if your tank carries a high load of animal life, and many tanks usually do.**

Protein Skimmers, or skimmers, as they are commonly called, are as important a component of a Reef Systems as the trickle filter itself. They are not, technically speaking, "filters", but let's not get too much into semantics.

Skimmers are mainly used to remove organic matter and free floating algae from the water, before they have a chance to break down, reduce the dissolved oxygen levels, and stress the biological filter in the process. Skimmers also remove some ortho-phosphates.

Proteinaceous matter resulting from excess food, undigested food, animal excretions, algae die-off, small life forms die-offs, etc... starts to break down in the tank water. Bacteria that are part of this process require oxygen and get it from the water, making less of it available to the other animals, including the bacteria in the trickle filter who need a lot of it themselves. This, in itself, is a first stress factor on all the tank's lifeforms, and on the filters (especially the biological filter).

The second stress factor results from the intermediate breakdown compounds produced during decay and mineralization. Many of these can be noxious, or stressful, at best. Some of these include : indoles, phenol, scatoles, organic acids, amines, nitrosamines, amides, etc. Preventing this protein matter from breaking down to begin with, prevents the formation of these intermediate compounds as well. The net result is less pollutants, less stress, and higher dissolved oxygen levels.

Naturally, even the best foam fractionators will not remove all proteinaceous matter from the water, neither will they remove all free floating microscopic and other algae. But they will remove a great deal of them. The best proof of their efficacy, the one I always like to point to, is the composition, and appearance, of the liquid-paste-like matter that collects in the skimmer cup. Just take a good look at it sometime. If you had not had a good and efficient skimmer, all of that material would still have been in the water, either as decomposed, or decomposing matter, producing numerous by-products in the process (and stress).

Since it is clear that skimmers are an efficient way of removing undesirable matter from the water, the only question that remains is how to size the skimmer correctly. Often, you are at the mercy of the manufacturer, and his recommendations, as to what unit is intended for your aquarium. These recommendations are often erroneous. At least that is what I have found, when trying different size skimmers on the same tank, to determine which model, size-wize, gave the best results.

Since the recommendations I referred to seem to be erroneous, where do they come from, and why are they given? I can only assume that they were arrived at by research at a time when Hobbyists kept mostly "fish-only" tanks, and that the recommendation only apply to such type aquariums. That would make sense, as it is unlikely that a manufacturer would knowingly give out wrong information.

Since the type of tank we are interested in is totally different from a load, maintenance and filtration standpoint, I would like to suggest that you disregard those recommendations, and look at the following table that was painstakingly arrived at over many many experiments, and then after you have done that, make your own judgment:

Factors influencing columnar skimming :
- diameter of tube or chamber.
- length of tube or chamber.
- type of airstone used (bubble size)
- amount of air blown into chamber

Factors influencing size of skimmer :
- size of aquarium.
- load of aquarium.
- feeding habits.
- maintenance and husbandry techniques.
- sophistication of filtration.

Of the 9 factors listed, some are beneficial and some are not. For example, using the right kind of airstone is a positive step, over-feeding is a negative one. Some factors are influenced by others, e.g. the sophistication of the filtration depends not only on having the right filter, but also the right pump, blowing air into the biological chamber, having fine filters in-line, etc.

It becomes quite complex, therefore, to decide on what type of skimmer to buy. Our recommendation is : when in doubt between two models, choose the larger one of the two.

We suggest that you decide between 5 "general" models :

- short and narrow diameter, 1 airstone.
- short and wide diameter, 2 airstones.
- tall and narrow diameter, 1 airstone.
- tall and wide diameter, 2 airstones
- venturi power protein skimmer, no airstones.

- Narrow is defined as three to four inches in diameter
- Wide is 6 inches or more
- Short is 18-20 inches of skimmer column (not total height)
- Tall is at least 36 inches of skimming height.

In the list that follows, circle the number of the situations that best applies to you, then add up all the numbers, or substract where minus figures are listed, if the situation applies to you. Once you have your total, refer to the recommendations at the end of this section as to which skimmer you should get. This is a fairly easy list to go through. If you do not want to write in the book, keep score on a separate sheet of paper.

Checklist for Sizing a Protein skimmer

(for tanks up to 125 gallons) :

- You have a trickle filter that meets the requirements outlined in this book (deduct 6)   –6
- You have a trickle filter that partially meets the requirements outlined in this book   3
- You are blowing a lot of air into the biological chamber   –1
- The air pump you are using is small, old and you have not recently changed the diaphragm   2
- Your are not blowing any air at all in the biological filter chamber   4
- You have no trickle filter   20
- You have a trickle filter with DLS (<6 months old)   4
- Your trickle filter contains DLS and is at least 6 months old   8
- Add 3 points to your score per 10 gallons of water in your system. Not including water in the sump.   ....
- Tank has a low biological load (be honest)   2
- Tank has a medium load   4
- Tank has a high load   8
- Tank has a very high load   15
- You are not using molecular absorption filters (6 discs or one pad per 25-30 gallons)   5
- You are using too few molecular absorption filters less than one per 25-30 gallons of water, but more than 1 per 50   2

- You are using about 6 M.A. discs, or one pad, per
25-30 gallons   –2
- You are not using activated carbon   2
- You clean your mechanical filters more than once a
week   –4
- You clean your mechanical filters at least once a week   –1
- You clean your mechanical filters about once every
2 weeks   5
- You clean your mechanical filters very infrequently   10
- You are not planning on using ozone   10
- You feed more than once a day   6
- You feed about 4 times a week   2
- You do not remove dead algae   4
- You use a Nitrate reducing compound   –6
- You do not use such a compound   4
- You are using a cartrige type mechanical filter, and
change it each time required   –3

Let us run through a few examples :

You have a 55 gallon tank, with trickle filter but it does not meet all the requirements outlined in this list, the load is medium, you feed 3 times a week and you plan to use ozone. 2 Poly Filters are used and so is X-nitrate. Your air pump is a fairly recent Schego, and your husbandry techniques are good. You clean all mechanical filters at least once a week : your score would be 26.5. If you were running the same tank without a trickle filter your score would be 49.5.

Same tank but with a heavy load, no Poly filters, and no X-nitrate and you do not really clean your mechanical filters every week : the score would be 42.5, and if you did not have a trickle filter, it would be 65.5 or more.

To decide on which skimmer is recommended for your tank, look at which category your total fits in :

- Up to 20 points : short and narrow
- 21 to 30 points : narrow and tall
- 31 to 49 points : wide and short
- 50 or more points : use a wide and tall, or a Venturi skimmer.

If you cannot find a skimmer of exactly the size recommended, it would be wise to buy a size larger than the recommendation. This will ensure that you have at least the amount of skimming that is, in my opinion, necessary.

Another way to use this checklist, is to determine which factors influence the skimmer size heavily, and then make sure you do not fall in that category. For example cleaning your mechanical filters at least once a week, and using ozone, takes a total of 20 points off your score.

Take the number of airstones we recommended into account as well, and remember that airstones need to be changed about every 3 to 4 weeks maximum. This will ensure that they always produce small bubbles, and skim more efficiently.

I strongly feel that a Reef tank needs to be run with a good and properly sized foam fractionator, protein skimmer. My experience, over and over, has been that its use results in greatly improved water quality, higher dissolved oxygen levels, and a higher **natural** redox potential.

Most Hobbyist will find that the protein skimmer they need will not fit underneath their aquarium cabinet. That may be one of the reasons they resort to either not using one, or using one that is too small. Such will, I feel, lead to problems with water quality, which in turn will lead to problems with the animals, and seemingly uncontrollable outbreaks of micro-algae, parasites and disease.

Skimmers can be hidden in special cabinets placed next to the tank, or if you are in the category that requires only a short and wide type, it may fit underneath a different type of cabinet. You may have to make the special cabinet yourself, or have it made at some local carpenter's work place. Another alternative is to use a Venturi skimmer, because they are smaller and "will" fit underneath the tank.

At the time of this writing only 3 types of Venturi skimmers were available in the North American market :

→ Tunze
→ Hippocampe – Klaes
→ Thiel•Aqua•Tech

Venturi skimmers tend to cost more money than columnar ones, but you will not need an airpump, and you also do not need air stones. Make sure that the model you decide on **can be operated with ozone**, as you will probably end up wanting to use it.

Determining the size of the protein skimmer and the number of airstones it should have, is only part of the equation. We still need to determine how much water to flow through the skimmer, and how much air should be used.

For every "load" there is an ideal flowrate, and that flowrate cannot be determined unless you have a redox controller. Since this is not a unit that we will include in a basic set up, we need to look for other ways of approximating that GPH,A and end up with an efficient skimmer. To do this, we need a few more explanations about protein skimmers.

As indicated already, the efficiency is determined by :
❏ Contact time of bubbles and water
❏ Size of the bubbles

But also by, in my opinion,
❏ materials used in the construction
❏ shape of the skimmer
❏ actual water level in the skimmer
❏ salinity of the water
❏ use of other additives

Air/Water Contact Time :

Tall skimmer columns obviously result in longer contact times. The water must travel downwards for longer, and the air must travel upwards for longer as well. The combination maximizes contact time.

World ClassAquarium
Brooklyn, New York. (718) 258 0653

A. Thiel says " Robert and Allan really know what they are doing "

Featuring the Add-On System for the person with an existing conventional salt water set up. This unit provides all the advantages of a wet-dry filter without the expense or hastle of breaking down the aquarium, drilling holes...

The heart of the system is the bio-filter unit which features a plexiglass drip plate, a dry chamber for bio media, and several wet chambers for chemical or other media. It is already used in schools, public aquariums and a university laboratory.

This is a most versatile unit, both in terms of media that can be used, and optional equipment such as skimmers, X-nitrate, sterilization, that very easily be added.

These Bio filters come in three sizes, holding respectively 9, 12 and 20 gallons of biological filtration media.

They will greatly improve the water quality, raise the dissolved oxygen levels, the natural redox potential, and living conditions for all lifeforms, including the most delicate corals and invertebrates.

Call us today for more details. Ask for Robert or Allan.

Equal flow rates through tall and short skimmers obviously result in different contact times. Water should be flowed slower through short skimmers to make it remain the skimmer longer, or it should be flowed faster, to increase the actual amount of times it goes through the skimmer. In my experience the first alternative works better.

Size of Air bubbles :

As already indicated, wooden airstones are still the best for fine bubbles. Lime wood is my preferred, although oak works better but requires a much stronger airpump, something most Hobbyists do not have. Wisa pumps, however, will blow through oak air stones.

We recommend you use limewood airstones, and change them every 3 weeks if you use ozone, and every 4 weeks if you do not. Although they used to be hard to get at one point, they are now plentiful.

I have also tried ceramic, bonded glass, porous polyethylene types, and although some of them do give off real fine bubbles, they are either not as small as those out of limewood, or you need an extremely powerful air pump, not something most Hobbyists have.

The exact amount of air that needs to be blown through the skimmer is very hard to determine and varies greatly. You may want to use the following guideline : blow as much air as is required to make the whole inside of the skimmer look like a milky white mass of water. Whisper 1000 air pumps, or similar will do the job in most cases. If you need a stronger pump, use a Wisa 100 or a 300, or 2 Whisper 1000's, one on each airstones (combine the output of the 2 air streams of each pump with a Tee and then connect it to each air inlet).

Shape of the Skimmer :

Most skimmers are built using round plastic tube (acrylic). The main reason for this shape, is that it provides an even and easy circular downflow of the water, from the top of the skimmer, where the water enters, to the bottom, where it exits. Circular flow increases the amount of time the water is actually in the skimmer column, and as a result better skimming is achieved.

This is by no means the only shape that one can use. My company makes 12 and 18 inch "square" protein skimmers for very large installation (several thousand gallons), that outperform round models, and cost considerably less. If properly constructed, such units are extremely efficient.

It is, however, a fact that most of the skimmers you will run accross, and that you will use, will be round. The water entry fitting should be angled in such a way, that the water is pumped sideways against the inside wall of the skimmer, and slightly downwards. This will ensure that the water rotates, and takes longer to get to the bottom of the skimmer.

Salinity of the Water :

Water of a higher salinity skims (foams) better than water of lower salinity. We have little choice over the salinity, as we have to stay within a very narrow range of 1.018 to 1.026 specific gravity. Most Hobbyists maintain their tanks at 1.023, which is also what most authors recommend. The point to remember is that skimming efficiency will diminish if you lower the salinity too much.

Water level in the skimmer :

The water level in the skimmer determines the type of foam that runs over the top, and into the collection cup of the skimmer. Wet foam, mostly plain water, is not properly skimmed water, and contains much less of the organic and other elements we wish to remove, than a dry foam, that is heavily concentrated, dark in color, and thick.

You must take care to regulate the height of the water in the column so as to obtain dry foam at the top, that runs over in to the cup from time to time. This may not be a one time task, as the way the water skims changes depending on salinity, load in the tank, feeding, etc. Skimmers must be monitored regularly, and adjusted from time to time to ensure optimum efficiency.

The color of the material that collects in the cup should be brown, green, black, or some dark color close to any of the three mentioned. Clear fluid, even if slightly yellowish, is not really what you want. Further adjustment of the skimmer's water level is necessary when that happens. Alternatively, try injecting more air, and/or changing the airstones. Often too, the fitting that you attach the hose to at the end of the airstone may need to be tightened more. If it is somewhat loose, not all the air goes through the wood. Some comes out directly, around the that fitting and forms large bubbles, reducing skimming efficiency.

Water Additives Used :

Many water additives will change the way in which the water foams. Some can really make the skimmer get totally out of hand. Such foam is mostly water that does not contains the extra material that you want to skim out of the tank.

Before using any additives, it is important that you try out a very small amount of them, to ensure that you will not have to re-adjust the skimmer. Many products, unfortunately, fall into this category. Running a skimmer with 6 or more inches of very wet foam at the top is counter productive. If you must use these elements, switch the skimmer off for a while (several hours, to over a day for some).

Certain trace elements will not make your skimmer foam more than it normally does. One such products is sold by T•A•T, but there are others.

■ Optimum Water flow :

Once you understand what will affect the operation of your skimmer, and made the necessary adjustments, you are ready to optimize the amount of water flowing through the skimmer. We assume, for this example, that you have followed the checklist, and that you have the right kind of skimmer, the one suggested and recommended for the type of tank that you keep.

• Take a small jar that can be closed airtight. The latter is very important. You must be able to fill it, and close it so no air whatsoever can enter the jar.
• Perform a dissolved oxygen test. Note the result.

• At the same time as you take water for your dissolved oxygen test, fill another jar completely, making sure that no air is trapped in the container.

• Store this jar with the water for 48 hours, in DARK place.

• Flow the content of the aquarium once, per hour, through the skimmer. For ease of calculations use the rated content of your tank.

• Let the skimmer run for 48 hours.

• Perform a dissolved oxygen test on the tank water, and a dissolved oxygen test on the water you stored.

• Compare the results of the the oxygen test you did two days ago with the one you just did. If it is lower, you are not skimming enough, and either your skimmer is too small, or your load is too high.

• Now test the water you put away for 48 hours. Compare the result with the Dissolved oxygen level you had the day you took this sample. Write down the difference.

• Refill the jar with aquarium water, and store for 48 hours.

• After 48 hours test the sample. Write the number down.

• Compare this result with the one you got when you took the sample. Note the difference.

• If you are running enough water through your skimmer the oxygen deficit should have gone down.

To illustrate this :

Flow rate	Day	D.O.	D.O.(48)	Difference
1 x tank	1	6.80	4.50	2.30
	3	7.00	4.80	2.20

At the above flow rate your tank's organic load went down; the skimmer removed it. How do we know that ? By looking at the dissolved oxygen (48) numbers, and comparing the first one you had with the second set. We are not interested as much in total dissolved oxygen, as in the difference between the first and second number. Notice that for the first set the difference was 2.30 (the deficit), and in the second set it was only 2.20, slightly less. Not much, but still slightly less.

Another example :

Flow rate	Day	D.O.	D.O.(48)	Difference
1.2 x tank	3	7.00	4.80	2.20
	5	7.20	5.60	1.60
1.5 x tank	7	7.50	6.20	1.30

All numbers in mg/l. Numbers were achieved on a 40 gallon reef tank, using a 30" x 6" skimmer from Thiel•Aqua•Tech. Tank had a heavy load of fish and invertebrates.

What you now want to do, is to change the flow rate through the skimmer and determine at which level, the difference between the D.O. test, and the test done on water taken at the same time, but stored for 48 hours, is the smallest. At that level the skimmer is removing the most organic material, and is running more efficiently. The reason for this is, that the higher the organic load left, the more oxygen will be consumed by bacteria in the 48 hour elapsed period, the greater the difference in the D.O. levels will be as well.

This may not be the quickest way to determine optimum flow rates, but it is certainly a method that is both easy and inexpensive, does not require elaborate equipment, and can be used by any Hobbyist.

Protein skimming is a special form of filtration, and the name is a misnomer. Skimming removes more than just organics (protein). Trace Elements, vitamins, fertilizer, and other elements will be removed as well. You must be aware of this, and replace these elements on a regular basis, lest you will run a tank with a deficit of beneficial compounds.

How much you should add is very hard to know, but add you must. Refer to the recommendations made by the manufacturers of the products that you use. If, in addition to a protein skimmer, you also inject ozone, you will need to add even more additives, as ozone breaks these compounds down rather quickly.

If you happen to be in the market for a skimmer and a filter, consider buying a trickle filter that incorporates a Venturi skimmer. Your total expenditure will be less, and you will have a skimmer that not only fits underneath the tank, but that works as efficiently as a 4 foot column (applies to T•A•T models).

Keep the following in mind when selecting and running an outside skimmer:
- Size the unit properly. Use the checklist as a guide.
- Change the airstones every 3 to 4 weeks.

- Adjust the water level so you produce only dry foam.
- Try to determine the optimum flow level.
- If you don't, flow 1.25 to 1.5 times the tank's content through the skimmer.
- Empty the cup regularly, or make it run into a bucket that you then empty.
- Adjust the water level in the skimmer as needed. This means and we have said it already, monitor your skimmer on a regular basis.

■ Venturi Skimmers :

Recently, more efficient and more compact protein skimmers, foam fractionators, have appeared on the market. Of the three models that were available at the time of this writing, only one was made in the United States.

Venturi skimmers do not require an air pump, but can be operated with one if you want to. The principle behind these skimmers has been around for along time. As water is forced through a special fitting, a differential pressure is created, and this differential pressure sucks air into the water stream, and breaks the air up in very small bubbles, giving the efficient skimming we instanced.

The more forceful the water is pushed through the Venturi valve, the greater the differential pressure, and the more air is being sucked in. Water flow levels needed vary, depending on which Venturi skimmer you purchase.

It may happen that the pump you are using to run your Venturi skimmer, is not pushing enough water through the Venturi. As a result not enough air for efficient skimming is being pulled in, and you have the impression that your unit is not working properly. There are two ways around this : one, push more water through the Venturi, and if that is not possible; two, attach a strong air pump to the intake of the Venturi valve and blow air into it. This will compensate for the lack of high water flow.

Venturi skimmers are appealing to many Hobbyists because they are compact, and will fit underneath the aquarium cabinet. If you plan to use ozone with such a skimmer, make sure that the unit you are planning to acquire can function with it. Some cannot, as a lot of Hobbyists have found out.

A Venturi skimmer's efficiency is determined by the quality of the "venturi" valve, and how it is constructed. Ideally it should have a Pitot tube inside. If not, the venturi still works, but may not draw air in as forcefully.

More details on "Pitot" tubes can be found in Advanced Reef Keeping Made Simple. Regardless of whether your skimmer has such a tube or not, more air can always be blown into the skimmer by means of a strong air pump, if such is necessary. Remember: the amount of water going through the skimmer is important, but what is more important is whether or not the skimmer operates efficiently, and that is determined by the mixture of air/water, and the size of the bubbles you generate. Some companies, e.g. Thiel•Aqua•Tech uses both "molded" and hand made Venturi valves. Molded valves obviously are more efficient but are more expensive.

If you have to make a choice between a columnar and a Venturi skimmer, the Venturi model will, in most cases, outperform the columnar one, especially if it is equipped with a molded venturi.

■ Conversion and Hang-on Units (Biological filters)

Several manufacturers now offer so-called conversion units, mostly geared towards the smaller tank, e.g. the 30 to 70 gallon range. Many will perform an excellent job for your aquarium, as long as you select the correct size for the tank you have, and the load you will keep.

What is most important in those units, is that the water is dispersed very evenly over **all** of the biological materials inside. Because you have less of it, you must use it more efficiently. This is where drip plates with many small holes are a must. It is probably best to actually "see" the unit before you buy it. Look through the magazines as well. Pictures can tell a lot too. One really excellent unit is made by World Class Aquarium, of Brooklyn, New York.

Several commercial units are available. Moe (1989) describes how you can make one yourself in "The Marine Aquarium Reference". That 500+ pages book contains a wealth of such information, and is well worth the investment of around 22.00 dollars. Look through the magazines, or at your local Pet Store, and you will usually find a selection of them.

Because of the reduced size these filters do not necessarily accommodate all of the extras that we have recommended earlier in this book. Select one that has as many as you can find, and supplement the system with additional filtration means, e.g. canister filters filled with Poly Filters, activated carbon, X-nitrate, or similar products that we have already described.

In these filters we recommend that you use plastic filtering material that definitely does not trap dirst. Since this is a smaller filter, you certainly do not want to have to clean it and destroy a great deal of bacteria in the process. Cubes, Blocs, Spheres, Techs, Balls, Packs, disks, and the newer Super•Techs will work well. Blocks and Cubes are especially well suited.

Remember : you must blow air into the biological chamber as this will greatly improve the efficiency of your filter. The biological processes that take place in the bio-chamber require a great deal of oxygen, because the bacteria that "perform the work" are aerobic. Not blowing air into the filter is, to make an analogy, like driving your car in third gear and never moving up to fourth or fifth, or, back to our filter, only using part of the available biological activity of the filter.

Make sure too that the conversion unit is of the "trickle" type, and not a submersed biomedia type. Although the latter units work too, of course, they operate at much lower levels of biological activity than the other types.

2. Water Sources, Uses and Treatment

■ Introduction

Up to this point, we have spent the greater part of this book talking about how to maintain the water quality necessary to keep invertebrates, corals, fish and other lifeforms normally added to Reef Tanks, in much better than average shape and condition. We have not said a word yet about the water itself and its sources, before it is added to the tank. Neither have we said anything about how water can, or should, be treated before it is used for the marine and reef aquarium.

Besides using it to fill their tanks, Hobbyists use water for the following three main purposes :
- to add water, when water changes are made,
- to regularly replenish evaporated water,
- when diluting water additives e.g. carbonate hardness liquids, trace elements, kalkwasser (limewater) vitamins, etc.

Whatever its purpose, the water used should be of superior quality. What the latter means, and I have not seen it defined frequently, is that all toxic and all unwanted matter, compounds, elements, or whatever they may be called, should have been removed through some process or another, prior to the water being used. In most cases it is the Hobbyist who decides which cleaning process will be used. I say in most cases, because a number of Hobbyists do not cleanse the water themselves, rather they buy water that has already been treated (e.g. distilled, or purified as it is now called by the USP) either from a Pet Store, or from some other supplier.

It is important to understand that "ensuring that the water used is of good quality", is a most consequential part of good tank maintenance. Indeed, once the water is in the tank, Hobbyists spend untold hours, and money, trying to ensure that it remains of good quality. Adding bad, or inferior, quality water to begin with, does, therefore, not make sense at all, especially when you consider the efforts and money spent to upgrade, and maintain, the quality of the water once the tank is up and running, and contains a lot of expensive and precarious livestock to boot.

As we shall see later in this chapter, there are many ways to purify, cleanse, or simply said "clean up" water before it is added to the Reef, or fish tank. More important than which exact form of purification is used, is the fact that some form "is". And let me say right away that you do not have to get extremely fancy either, to get good water quality. There are many ways to do so that are both inexpensive, and efficient, in terms of the effluent water produced.

■ Water Sources

Freshwater sources are the most commonly used ones for the purposes already mentioned, and include the following:

- tap water
- well water
- lake water
- river water
- distilled or purified bottled water
- mineral water (bottled)
- spring water (bottled)
- de-ionized water from outside vendors (bottles, bags)
- reverse osmosis water from outside vendors
- some even use or have access to lab quality water.

Purified seawater sources are not as frequently used, but are available in certain parts of the country. This is, of course, an excellent supply source, and its use should be encouraged. Unfortunately not many Hobbyists are lucky enough to have it available. If you do, consider using it on a regular basis, or from time to time. You may, for example, not wish to use it to perform all water changes, but you could, to keep costs down, use it every other time, or every third (etc.) time. Because of its "completeness" it is hard to beat its quality.

Freshwater Supply Bottle or similar container

Must be airtight   **Not to Scale**

Small I.D. hose

Water Level in Sump

Sump   Pump (to tank)

Biological Chamber of filter not shown

■ Water Uses

✓ Top-Offs :

replenishing evaporated water with cleansed "freshwater" is a task no Hobbyist can avoid, as no one has control over evaporation. **Drip systems** that operate on the "water level in the sump basis" are simple to install, and should be used if at all possible. They are very inexpensive, and can be easily home made.

The diagram at the top of this page shows such a system.

Note the following about its operation :

• the freshwater bottle, or canister, must be "airtight". This is most important, as if it is not, the bottle will empty itself in a matter of minutes or even less.

• the principle behind this system is the same as the well known water dispenser in offices, where a large, usually 5 gallon, bottle sits upside down in the dispenser. As you push the manifold, water comes out of the spout. As the level inside the dispenser becomes lower than the bottom of the neck of the upside down bottle, air gets in the bottle, and water comes out, until the end of the neck of the bottle touches the water again. You can notice this happening when air suddenly rushes in the upside down bottle (while water gets out at the same time, and refills the reserve container inside the water dispenser).

• in this system the principle is exactly the same. As the end of the small internal diameter tubing is less immersed, because of evaporation, it will eventually be slightly out of the water. This lets air in, and water out of the reserve container, and achieves the desired result of adding water to the sump.

• the container, or bottle, must be rigid, so it will not crush as the vacuum inside of it becomes greater as it empties itself. Rigidness is most important, or your system will not work. If the container collapses on itself, all water will come out and be added to the system. Not what you are trying to do.

• use small internal diameter hose : 1/4 to 3/8 inch will work fine. Smaller may not work in all cases (especially if the run is long, and the container small). Rigid hose, or small diameter pipe will work even better. I use 3/8 internal diameter pvc pipe.

• Attach the bottle or canister with some sort of bracket, so it can not move up or down.

• Replenish the bottle whenever required. The larger the bottle or container is to begin with, the less often you will have to do so.

Alternatively you can, of course, as many Hobbyists do, perform the top-offs **manually**, adding the necessary amount of replacement water by hand. Make some sort of a mark on the side of the trickle filter sump, so you know where the level should be, and when it is not, add the required amount of "treated" water. Adding raw water, for example from the tap, can be done, but only if you are sure that that water is safe to use on your tank. This can only be determined by testing it extensively, something the average Hobbyist cannot do, or normally does not do.

To play it safe, treat the water by running it through some form of chemical filtration medium. I recommend Poly Filters® from Poly Bio Marine, or molecular absorption discs from the same company highly, and use them myself all the time.

Certain manufacturers sell small dosing pumps that will add water drop-wize to your tank. Two such companies are Tunze and my own. A small dosing pump to add drops should not cost you more than $160.00. The device can also be used, of course, for adding certain additives at the same time. Not all types of pumps can handle all types of additives (e.g. compounds that contain particulates cannot be dispensed with small diameter peristaltic pumps, as the tubing would soon loose its vacuum, making the pump inoperative).

I also use a pump to add "Kalkwasser", meaning limewater, drop-wize to the Reef, to maintain a high calcium hardness (not the same as carbonate hardness). This greatly benefits my corals and also results in red, pink, purple and greyish coralline algae growing all over the aquarium. This a diaphragm type pump, not a peristaltic one.

If the doser pump (often a small peristaltic pump) that you use delivers more than the amount of water that you want to add to your tank, all you need to do is to run it for a lesser number of hours (not 24 hours, round the clock). Do so by using a timer. Radio Shack sells really excellent Micronta brand timers that are inexpensive, and will do the job just fine.

It is also recommended to place a small airstone in the container that holds the water from which the doser is pumping, and run a small amount of air through it. This is especially handy if you dispense a mixture of compounds, as it will keep all parts in solution, and prevent the heavier ones from settling to the bottom (for example, calcium, vitamins, and some fertilizers).

If yours is the physical manual system of topping off, add the water slowly, and preferably to the sump of the trickle filter, not to the tank itself. It will mix better in that fashion. Top-off frequently, perhaps every day or every other day, if necessary.

Simpler Drip Systems :
Yet another way to top-off your tank is with a simple drip system, adjusted to deliver the quantity of freshwater that you need every day. This spreads the amount added evenly throughout the day and keeps conditions really stable in the tank. All you will need is a reserve vat, at piece of airline tubing, and a small clamp to adjust the flow. Start up the syphon effect, adjust the flow, and your drip systems is up an running. Slow drip systems can be somewhat tricky to adjust. Because the tubing out of which the water is coming is very restricted, they may stop. Frequent adjustments may therefore be necessary. Try it, and if it is too cumbersome for you to deal with, resort to some other method described here.

✓ Water Changes :

There are many differing theories on water changes. Some go as far as to advocate that with "their" systems no water changes whatsoever are necessary, ever. This may have been true for them, but it has never worked for me. Some form of water changing seems necessary, regardless of how sophisticated your system becomes. I have said so for many years, and to date, even with all the sophistication of my own tanks, I am still convinced that water changes are a must.

Since this book is dedicated to the small reef tank, I definitely recommend that you perform water changes on a regular basis. I have long held the theory, based on my own experience, that the best results are obtained when water changes are both :

• frequent   and   • small

rather than infrequent and large. The reason for that is simple: small and frequent water changes do not change the water composition (chemistry) as much as large ones do, putting less stress on the fish, corals and invertebrates. The changes referred to include temperature, pH, salinity, osmotic pressure, ionic balance, percentage make-up of minerals and individual chemical elements, and so on. You would be amazed what a 20 or 25 percent water change can do to those conditions !

I have, for years, recommended that you change 4 to 5 percent of the tank's water per week, or 2 to 2.5 percent every 3 days. This is simple to do for most Hobbyists, as it normally does not involve handling a great deal of water. For example, if you have a 55 gallon tank, change about 2.5 to 3 gallons a week, or about one gallon every 3 days. Don't bother being totally "accurate", round the numbers off so they match some known container that you use (bucket, jar, old plastic water bottle, etcetera). Small water changes have one more benefit : you are less likely to make a mess by spilling water.

Additionally things cannot get out of hand that much either, because you perform water changes every couple of days. As a result, noxious elements cannot accumulate to any degree, and pollution is much less likely to be present in such amounts that it would cause undue stress on the tank lifeforms. Examples of this include phosphates and nitrates, to name just two.

How do you change water ?

Manually is the most frequently used method. Remove the amount that you are going to replace first, then add the new water slowly, and preferably to the sump of the trickle filter.

It cannot be stressed enough that both salinity and temperature need to be adjusted beforehand. Perhaps, because we are dealing with a small amount of water, exact, precise, adjustments are not required, but the salinity and temperature must be approximately the same, as those of the water in the tank. You do not want to add water at a temperature that is much much colder, or much much warmer. If the difference is only a degree or so, and the water is added to the sump, no harm will be done. The same applies to salinity, although in this case, you do not have as much latitude. Best is to keep the differences as small as you can.

Use water from a vat where it was prepared beforehand. Do not make up the mixture right then and there. If you do, all of the salt will not be dissolved properly, and adding such water to your tank will lower the redox potential of your aquarium quickly and drastically, stressing all lifeforms in the tank. I have seen the redox potential go down by over 100 mv several times, during testing (Thiel Lab. Bk 23).

Keep the recommendation made earlier in mind. Change small amounts of water frequently, not large amounts infrequently. Change water on a regular schedule, and stick to that schedule. It will be easier for you to remember to do so, for instance, if you always perform your water changes on, say, Fridays or Saturdays.

Automatic water changers are now being installed more and more frequently , and are both simple to set up, and inexpensive to acquire. Check the diagram below for more information :

Notes of importance :

• To install an automatic water changer, you need to be able to drain the excess water that will accumulate. This requires either that it flow into a vat of some sort, to a water drain in the floor, or to a sink (by means of a small pump and hose or pipe).

• Since, more than likely, only a very small amount of water, will need to be changed, you will only need a very low output pump. That

AUTOMATIC WATER CHANGER SUGGESTIONS AND OPTIONS

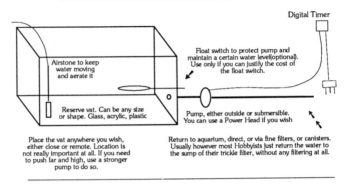

is the reason a power head type pump can easily be used. Often even the smallest ones will do.

• I recommend using a digital timer. Such timers can be set to trigger at on/off cycles of very short intervals, for example, 1 or 2 or 3 minutes. Mechanical timers usually work only in 15 or 20 minute intervals. Letting the pump run for that long may move more water than you want to, especially if you keep a small tank. Indeed, if you have a 55 gallon tank for example, and you wish to change 1 percent of the water per day, you will want to change only 0.55 gallons, meaning about half a gallon. That is not very much, and only very small pumps, running for a very short amount of time will allow you to do so.

If your pump still moves too much water, notwithstanding the digital timer's setting to its minimum cycle (usually 1 minute), put a C-clamp on the output hose of the pump or power head, and close it gradually more and more, until the right amount of water is moved from the reserve vat to the tank (or sump), in the minimum on/off cycle your timer allows. In fact, anything that restricts the output of the pump, respectively power head, used, will do the job. Small ball valves, shut-off valves, and the like can be used, but be sure that they contain no metal parts, except 316 SS.

• I suggest that you do place an airstone in the reserve vat to keep the water moving around. This will keep it properly mixed and also oxygenated. Water reserve vats must be cleaned from time to time. I suggest at least once a month. This will prevent sediment from accumulating, and possibly breaking down into undesirable compounds.

• Since this is "water-changing" water, it has to be prepared first, and salt added. Preferably use a salt that is low in phosphates, nitrates, and other impurities. Most nationally sold brands are excellent of course. We use Tech•Reef Salt and Hawaiian Marine Mix on an alternating basis, and supplement with Reef•Elements, Vita•Trace, KSM, Iodine Supplement, and the new "Tech•Liquid•Gold" very special nutrient for fish and corals.

Gravity feed water changers

Place a vat with prepared salt water higher than the tank, or higher than the sump of the trickle filter. This will allow it to gravity feed downwards.

Attach a small diameter hose to the vat and guide it to the sump. Install a solenoid valve and a timer (as shown in the diagram). Set the time for minimum on/off cycling, clamp the output hose down until only as much water is delivered as you actually want to change. The diagram shows exactly how to set such a system up.

Solenoids can be obtained from companies dealing with fluid processing, scientific supply places, and some plumbing supply companies. One company that offers a large selection of 110 volt, 2-way solenoids is Richdel/Garden Centers, in Carson City, Nevada. Another source is W. W. Graingers.

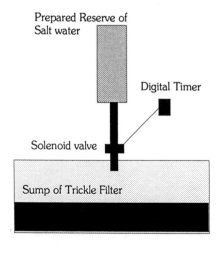

Prepared Reserve of Salt water

Digital Timer

Solenoid valve

Sump of Trickle Filter

Such a system can easily be set up for under fifty dollars. Digital timers of excellent quality can be bought at Radio Shack and similar places.

Make sure that the solenoid valve does not have any metal other than 316 SS that come in contact with the salt water.

Drawing not to scale

Biological area of filter is not shown

Evacuating Water from the sump (if you do not have a floor drain to which it can be guided)

Even if you do not have a floor drain, you can still install an automatic water changer, providing you are prepared to take some time to install the required components seen in the diagram below (not to scale. May look complicated to set up, but is in reality not) :

All in all, your expenses will amount to the cost of a float switch and a power head (which you may already have). You must use a float switch that allows you to control a "high" level, not a "low" level (the type used to protect pumps and prevent them from running dry).

Water Changer Water evacuation from the Sump

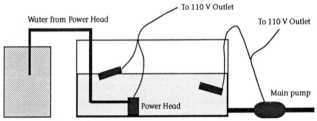

Vat to collect excess water, each time water changer works. Instead of pumping to a vat, you can pump to a sink as well (much better of course, since you will not have to empty the vat all the time.

Sump of Trickle filter with 2 Float switches. One controls the main pump, the other one switches on a smaller inside pump, e.g. a power head, when the level inside the sump rises above a level you determine yourself.

Best, of course, would be to evacuate the water that the power head or small pump, is removing from the sump, directly to a sink. If you use a vat, use a large one, so you do not have to empty it all the time. Adjust the level at which the float switch triggers, over a few trial and error sessions, until you are satisfied it does so at the correct level.

As water is added by the water changer, the level in the sump will rise, since more water is now in the "system". This extra water will collect in the sump.

The float switch attached to the power head senses a higher water level, and triggers the power head (or small pump) to start pumping water out of the trickle filter's sump. This water is then collected in another vat, or guided directly to a sink by means of flexible hose.

■ Treating the Water before it is used

✓ Mechanically

Mechanical filters are meant to remove dirt, detritus, particulate matter, debris, etc. from the water before it is being treated further. You are familiar with mechanical filters, because you already use them on the tank itself. They are often referred to as fine filters or pre-filters.

A canister filled tightly with filter floss, or some similar material will do the trick for rough type impurities. If you want to filter down to the smaller material you will have to resort to the use of filter cartridges.

Such cartridges do a fine job, but the cost of using them can creep up on you quickly. You are probably acquainted with "micron" filters, rated in values such as 100, 75, 50, 25, 10, 5, 1 and some even less than one micron. Keep the following in mind when selecting a micron cartridge of any type of rating : there are two types, referred to as "nominal" and "absolute".

Absolute means the cartridge does not let any material larger than the rating through, nominal lets some through. For example, a 50 micron nominal cartridge will let some 60, 70, etc. material through; an absolute 50 micron cartridge will not. Absolute rated cartridges are quite more expensive than nominal ones. If you plan on using this type of mechanical filtration, stick with nominal rated cartridges.

One advantage of using "very small particulate" filters, is that they remove not only debris, but also parasites, bacteria etc. To do so, however, you will need to use special sub-micron filters (<than 1 micron). This is also called cold sterilizing.

The smaller the rating of the cartridges, the faster they will clog up, unless you place several of them in series, starting with the highest. A series of 100, then 50, then 25, then 10, then 5, will give excellent results, but is much too expensive to set up for our purposes, especially in a "basic" Reef.

Whether or not you need to pre-filter, or fine filter the water you will be using, often depends on the source of the water itself. Tap water and well water, will contain few "visible" particles, but keep in mind that even with good eye sight, you will not see debris smaller than 40-50 microns.

Certain areas of the country have water that contains considerable amounts of debris, of all forms, and it is recommended to pre-filter the water if such is your case. If you buy a filter assembly to do so in a do-it-yourself type store, look for "rust and debris" canister filters. They usually cost between 30.00 and 40.00 dollars, and replacement cartridges can be bought for around 5.00.

Anyone with well water should pre-filter as well, especially because of usually high amounts of undissolved mineral and other compounds it contains. Use the same filter type as if you were removing rust and debris from tap water.

Plain sand filters will remove a fair amount of debris as well, and are easy to set up. All you need is an old aquarium, some sand and flexible hose. The diagram below shows exactly how to set such a filter up.

Sand Filter for Fine Filtration

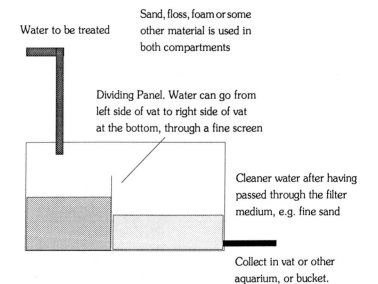

Water to be treated

Sand, floss, foam or some other material is used in both compartments

Dividing Panel. Water can go from left side of vat to right side of vat at the bottom, through a fine screen

Cleaner water after having passed through the filter medium, e.g. fine sand

Collect in vat or other aquarium, or bucket.

A simpler system yet, would be to use two buckets, one sitting on top of the second one. The first one has a perforated bottom over which plastic screening material is laid. This is then covered with sand, or filter floss, or foam, or some other material that allows fine filtering. The water goes through the material in the first bucket and drips, respectively flows, into the second one, cleaner and mechanically filtered. This is, for sure, the least expensive way to set up a mechanical filter, but it is not to be considered a low micron filter. It will remove gross impurities, and some finer as well, especially if you use a thick layer of fine sand.

Remember to rinse the sand after each session. Let it dry in a flat tray to prevent the formation of anaerobics. If you do not let it dry, rinse it each time before you use it. This is simpler, and is probably what most Hobbyists will do.

These filters can be made more efficient by flowing the water through layers of progressively finer, and finer, filtering material. The coarser layers remove the larger material, and the progressively smaller ones are removed as the water has to go through smaller (finer) filtering media. Both Moe (1982) and Spotte (1976) give more details on such filters.

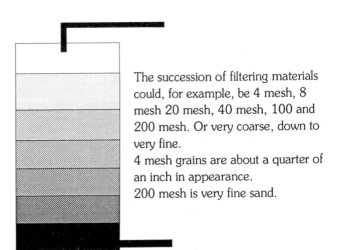

The succession of filtering materials could, for example, be 4 mesh, 8 mesh 20 mesh, 40 mesh, 100 and 200 mesh. Or very coarse, down to very fine.
4 mesh grains are about a quarter of an inch in appearance.
200 mesh is very fine sand.

Remark : fine filters such as these do not remove dissolved material, e.g. phosphates and nitrates. To do this you will need a totally different filter, described later in this section.

The example uses different mesh sizes of gravel and sand, to go from very coarse to very fine. Between uses, the filter should be allowed to drain. Before collecting water for use in the tank, the system should be run for a few minutes to remove any possible anaerobic contamination. If you wish, you can place filter floss between each layer to keep them separated, although that is not really necessary.

✓ Activated Carbon filters

Moe (1989) states that chemical filtration, of which activated carbon is but one example, is in fact mechanical filtration on a molecular basis. Chemical filters, indeed, remove "dissolved" material at the molecular level. The chemical filters described earlier, remove "undissolved" material.

A.C., or activated carbon has been around in the hobby for a long time. Unfortunately my experience with such A.C. is not good at all, except for a few brands that use the better quality material, especially the more expensive varieties.

Plan on using the latter if you include A.C. filtration in your pre-use treatment of the water. Don't waste your money on a product that may add more undesirable matter to the water, than there already is. One such compound frequently added is "phosphate" in many forms. Phosphate is the cause of many problems in the tank, and leads to the appearance of micro-algae, often in uncontrollable quantities, that can quickly "ruin" an otherwize fine looking aquarium. These low quality carbons (some not even activated) should be avoided at all cost. Foreign imports too, should be tested before use in the tank, as I have had several bad experiences with 2 types, and have lost corals as a result.

What determines the quality of the carbon, is the source of the base material to make it, and the fabrication process used. This gives rise to the existence of the following main types of activated carbon:
- charcoal
- bituminous carbon
- lignite carbon
- coconut shell carbon (sometimes called vegetable base)
- mixtures of the above, or "non-descript" origins of carbon material, e.g. bone, some woods, and others.

Any type of carbon can provide excellent results in certain specific applications. This is also the reason why every manufacturer can claim that their carbon is just "the" best. It turns out, however, that in aquarium use "the" best for another application, may not be adequate for what we are trying to do, keeping a vibrant looking reef tank.

Many carbons leach phosphate into the water, a fact first pointed out to me by Ken Howery, and further confirmed by personal testing, and the results of tests made by readers of Marine Reef, the newsletter published by Aardvark Press.

Because phosphates are at the source of many micro-algae problems in Reef and other tanks, we must at all cost avoid adding more phosphate to the water. In fact, we should do all possible to remove PO_4 through whatever means we can.

Ortho-Phosphate, organic phosphate, nitrate, ammonia, nitrite, phenol, volatile organic compounds, amines, and many other chemicals that are undesirable can be present in incoming water, whether it be tap, or well. Additionally, tap water can often contain high amounts of chlorine, and sometimes chloramine and hexametaphosphate as well. All of the latter need to be removed, before that water can safely be used and added to the reef tank (and fish-only tanks as well of course).

Activated carbon of good quality will remove most of the above compounds (there are better methods as we shall see a little later) and neutralizes chlorine as well. It should, therefore, be considered in a set up to pre-treat tap and well water, and not overlooked completely. There are excellent carbons available.

For a much more in depth explanation on the differences between the various forms of chemical filtation, e.g. ion exchange, adsorption, absorption, molecular sieves, reverse osmosis, tangential flow filters, and so on, read Moe (1989) The Marine Aquarium Reference, published by Green Turtle Press, a book all Reef Keeping Hobbyists should have, and read.

Based on what we have seen so far, a filter to pre-treat the water could look as follows (there are many variations) :

The 2 component unit shown can be improved upon by using a canister that can be set up with both carbon, and diatomaceous earth. Such a canister will remove whatever A.C. removes, and will filter down to very low micron levels. Unfortunately my experiences with diatomaceous earth filters do not let me recommend this set-up. You could however consider a System 1™ micron filter set-up, with powdered activated carbon.

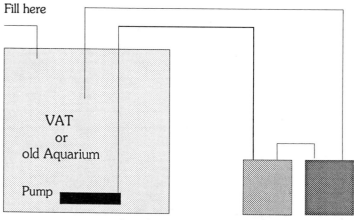

Fill here

VAT
or
old Aquarium

Pump

Simple re-circulating set-up

The above system pulls water from the vat or old aquarium, circulates it through a first and then a second canister, and then back to the vat. Water from a well or tap is used to fill the vat. The system, once switched on, can recirculate without the Hobbyist having to stand around. Fill one canister with a good quality activated carbon, and the second one with sand, or floss, or a similar mechanical filtration medium. This simple system will give you better quality water than you would have if you did not treat at all, but can still be improved upon as we shall see in this chapter.

Such filters are advertised in the magazines you read, and are worth looking into, as they allow you to combine two filtration steps in one unit. When you now supplement this with the next one that we recommend, you will then have a complete pre-filtration system that cleans the water more than adequately for use in your Reef aquarium. Activated carbon is also used in the system's filtration, especially to control residual ozone. See previous chapters for more details.

✓ Molecular Absorption Filters :

My favorite form of filtration, because it removes more from the water than activated carbon does, can be visually inspected easily, does not leach anything back into the water, and is cost efficient to boot.

Molecular absorption filters come in pad form, or in discs, and are manufactured, and sold, by the Poly-Bio-Marine Company through distributors only. There are, however, so many of them that you should not have any problems finding "Poly Filters" or discs in your area. If you have not tried them yet, you definitely should.

I recommended already that you use them in your actual system filtration. Now I would like you to make them part of your pre-filtration stage as well. This is the last component of an efficient filtration set-up.

The set up I recommend for treating water before using it for your tank thus comprises three parts :

- • activated carbon for chlorine removal and some impurities
- • fine filtration for removing particulate matter
- • molecular absorption for final polishing of the water.

The effluent from such a system is just as good as what you would obtain from systems costing perhaps 5 to 6 times more, at least. Don't waste your money. In the type of tank we are concerned with in this book, you must use every dollar you are going to spend as wisely as possible, so you can include all the equipment that is recommended for a minimum set-up.

Because Poly Filters and discs change color as they progressively exhaust their absorption capability, it is easy to determine when they need to be replaced. For pre-filtration purposes, they should last quite some time. Many more months probably, if the water in your area is not of all that bad quality to begin with.

✓ Reverse Osmosis :

Although often seen advertised in Hobby magazines, and indeed an efficient way of purifying the water, I see reverse osmosis on the small tank as overkill, insomuch as the type of R.O. unit you require to do a good job, is expensive, and still the units are slow.

In addition, reverse osmosis filters waste a lot of water. At best, for every gallon of filtered water you end up with, you have, conservatively, wasted another four (more likely 6 or 7). Reverse osmosis filters are very slow, especially the units that are somewhat affordable. The smaller ones produce only 5 to 6 gallons per 24 hours.

What is also important to understand, is that the quality of the water comning out of the reverse osmosis unit is determined by the quality of the membrane used inside of it. The better the semi-permeable membrane used, the better the quality of the effluent water, but the more expensive the unit will become. Good reverse osmosis systems, the ones that produce so-called ultra pure water, can easily cost around one thousand dollars. Not nearly within the budget we have planned for the small reef tanks discussed in this book.

For those interested in what osmosis and reverse osmosis are all about, and how the actual system works, we refer you to the in-depth discussion on the subject by Moe (1989) in "The Marine Aquarium Reference, Systems and Invertebrates", Green Turtle Publications, (obtainable from Aardvark Press as well).

Reverse Osmosis filtration is efficient in producing high quality water, no doubt about it, but I strongly feel that we do not need such a set up in a small reef aquarium set up. If you already own such a filter, and if it was bought for prices around 100 to 200 dollars, you probably do not have all that good a unit, at least not of the quality just referred to. Check the effluent for nitrates, and especially for phosphates. Some ortho-phosphate may be left in the water, and organic phosphate will still be there as well. All is not wasted however.

If such is the case, the effluent may have to be treated again, or run through a different type of filter. We suggest that you use Poly Filters or discs. Also, if the reverse osmosis filter you are using lets such compounds through, you should consider doing away with it altogether and resorting to a less wasteful and more efficient method of pre-filtration, (see our suggestion later in this chapter). **Water "is" a precious commodity. Preserve it.**

✓ De-Ionization :

An excellent way of treating water before it is added to the tank. Very effective at producing highly purified water. There are a few problems associated with using such a resin set-up however, especially at the Hobbyist level.

Resins only have a limited ability to remove impurities; to clarify this means that they can only absorb-adsorb a certain amount of them, and then they become ineffective. View resins as highly porous materials that have an enormous internal surface area. When the surface area is filled so to speak, no further impurites can be removed from the water, and the resins stop working, and need to be cleaned.

That is where the problem starts, for most hobbyists anyway. To recharge resins, special treatments need to be performed, and these treatments require the use of rather strong chemicals. Not everyone is prepared to take the time to "re-charge", as it is called, the resins, and not everyone is prepared to handle the chemicals that are necessary to do so, either. Moreover, a lot of Hobbyists who are unfamiliar with chemicals, should not use them to begin with.

Although de-ionization is very effective, and certainly recommendable, we prefer you to stay away from it if you can. Resort to other methods, easier to implement, and not so cumbersome in their use, especially the regeneration part, which requires that you keep chemicals around that can be dangerous if not used properly, or if they fall into the hands of children, who do not know how about them, and could get seriously hurt as a result. I am not saying "do not use this process", but I am definitely alerting you to the potential problems that surround this form of water purification. In fact, because we sell de-ionizers at my company, and in light of what we have just said, we offer a re-charging service for resins, so Hobbyists do not have to do it themselves.

Again, these comments lead us to a simpler filtration set-up, one we will describe a little later in this chapter, and the one I use myself to prepare water for our tanks. I sometimes use de-ionization as well, but only if I need water for very special purposes, e.g. when testing chemicals that are used in products that my company manufactures, when I want to be sure the water we need, does not contain any elements that may interfere with the working of the various compounds and products being tested.

Resin filtration can take on many forms. Details can be found in my other books, and also in our Newsletter Marine Reef, Volume 1, Numbers 20 and 21. Dozens and dozens of different resins exist and are manufactured by many companies, Rohm and Haas being perhaps the best known one. Each resin, or each set of resins, as two are normally required, is meant to perform a specific task. To do the job, therefore, you need very specific resins, not just any type. This is often overlooked by the Hobbyist, or small manufacturer, who is eager to have a product, and does not invest in the necessary research to end up with the right resin for salt water reef tank applications.

Keep in mind too, that you cannot use de-ionizing resins in salt water. Ionic competition, especially from the compounds that are present in salt water in great quantities such as salt (sodium), interferes with the process. This coats the outside of the resins very quickly, and as a result, they become totally "blocked" so to speak, and do not perform the task you obtained them for anymore. You have, in essence, wasted your money, and may have a false sense of security, thinking that the resins are in fact cleaning your water.

✓ Ultra-Violet Sterilization :

UV sterilizers have been around for quite some time, and are meant to kill bacteria and other undesirable very small life forms in the water. As such, UV sterilizers can play a role in pre-treating the water.

Since I have already pointed out that a micron filter of a small rating can do the same job for you in a much easier fashion, my recommendation is that, if bacteria, protozoa and parasites are a concern, use a sub-micron filter. It is simple to install, easy to clean and maintain, and inexpensive on top of it.

Ultra-Violet Sterilization equipment also brings about a set of problems that need to be dealt with for the unit to operate efficiently. For example, the water must flow slowly through the housing, and very closely to the bulb itself; the latter must be jacketed in a quartz sleeve, for optimum efficiency, as quartz glass lets UV rays through.

The "wattage" of the bulb(s) must be accurately decided upon. Bulbs need to be changed frequently, and need to preferably operate at a temperature exceeding 100 degrees Fahrenheit. If operated at the temperature of the tank water, the bulb is nowhere near as efficient.

For pre-filtering water, this is not at all a practical solution, in my opinion, and I have therefore not included it in the suggested pre-filtering set-up discussed later.

✓ Ozonization as a pre-treatment :

If you treat great amounts of water at one time, and if you have cause to believe that bacteria, parasites, protozoa, etc. may be present in the water, ozonization is a viable form of pre-filtration.

Again, however, sub-micronic filters will do the same job for you, and in a simpler and less expensive manner, I believe.

If ozone is used, you must over-ozonize, and do so to a degree that you can definitely detect residual ozone in the water that is being treated. Use a strong unit. There are now several choices. Sander, and my own company are two. Spotte, in his "Seawater Aquariums" book, gives a detailed discussion on using ozone for this purpose.

Dry and cool the air going into the unit to maximize the amount of ozone generated, to obtain an efficient kill of small lifeforms, and to burn out (oxidize) organic material that will be present as a result.

Ozone can be used as an optional add-on to the system I recommend, and is shown in the diagram later in this chapter. Make sure that all residual ozone is removed from the water before it is added to the tank.

✓ Chemical Additives :

In areas where the water is highly polluted, some Hobbyists resort to the use of chemicals such as chlorine (in tablets) to pre-treat the water, they add permanganates and similar strong oxidizers, and then filter the water through a sub-micron filter and a chemical filter.

Although that is certainly a good method, I find it too elaborate and too difficult to implement for the average Hobbyist. Stay away from chemicals, unless you absolutely have to use them.

Make sure too, that they are removed from the water through some other form of filtration before you use the treated water for the tank. Permanganates will raise the redox potential to extremely high, and dangerous, levels. You must therefore let the water stand for quite some time and aerate it to counteract that effect. It must also be treated.

✓ Cold sterilization :

We have touched on this in the section on mechanical filtration. I highly recommend this form of pre-treatment because it is easy to install and does not pose any danger. It is inexpensive as well.

Use a filter material that is rated for less than one micron. You will thus remove not only particulate matter, but also bacteria, parasites and all protozoa that could pose problems for your Reef lifeforms.

It is included in the system that I use myself, and that is described a little later in this chapter. Many types are available, even at your local do-it-yourself- store, or hardware supply house. All you need to check is whether the cartridges, or filter bags, are rated for less than one micron, or not. Larger rated assemblies will not cold sterilize.

✓ Suggested Set-up for pre-filtration :

Based on what you have read so far, you are probably already aware of what is included in such a system :

- an activated carbon stage, mostly to remove chlorine
- a sub-micron stage, to remove particulate, bacteria, etc.
- a molecular absorption stage, to really polish the water
- a storage and aeration stage (if necessary)
- optional ozonization stage, including dryer and air pump.

In our case the system is piped into a main water line, but you can hook the whole assembly up by means of a hose to a faucet. Mount all filters on a small wooden platform with casters, and you can roll it around easily, to where you will need it. Clean the system, that is flush it, before each use, to remove the stagnating water. To do so, run water through the system for a few minutes. This will get out all water that is low in oxygen and may have started to decay, and provide clean and freshly filtered water for your system.

Change the carbon once a month, or sooner, depending on how much water you treat. Watch the color of the Poly Filters, or molecular absorption discs, and change them when needed.

Flow water through this system as slowly as you can. This ensures that you get high quality water, free of nitrate, phosphate and other contaminants in "one pass", meaning the water has to go through the filters only once.

Use old canister filters, or special filters such as the ones sold in D.I.Y. stores, to set the system up. Connections can be made with hose barbs, hose clamps, and flexible acrylic or vinyl hose. Never ever run tap water pressure on the system. Many canisters are not built to withstand that kind of "psi". First close the tap water off, and then the canisters, is a valve is installed at the end of the line. This is very important to remember.

Control the flow, meaning adjust the amount of water flowing through the system, from the beginning of the line, not the end. If you put an aquarium type canister under city water pressure, it will burst open and you will have a flood, and may get hurt.

You may also wish to combine the three types of filtration somewhat. I already indicated that powdered activated carbon, and fine filtration, can be combined into one unit, by using, for example, a System 1™ filter. Add an extra canister filled with the Poly filters, or molecular absorption discs, in line, and you have an inexpensive system that will perform very well for you.

Rather than using a one-pass system such as the one shown, you can also use a re-circulating system. Draw water from an old aquarium, or any type of container, and recirculate it through the filter system that you have set up, and back to the original container. Let everything run for 10 to 15 minutes, or less, depending on how much water you are in fact treating.

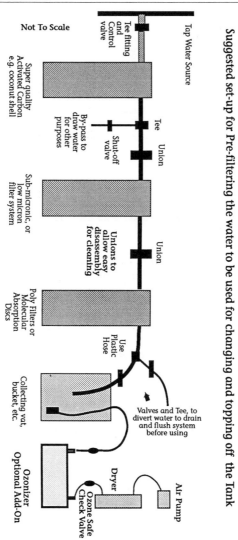

Suggested set-up for Pre-filtering the water to be used for changing and topping off the Tank

Not To Scale

Tap Water Source

Tee fitting and Control valve

Super quality Activated Carbon e.g. coconut shell

By-pass to draw water for other purposes

Tee

Shut-off valve

Union

Sub-micronic, or low micron filter system

Unions to allow easy disassembly for cleaning

Union

Poly Filters or Molecular Absorption Discs

Use Plastic Hose

Collecting vat, bucket, etc.

Valves and Tee, to divert water to drain and flush system before using

Ozonizer Optional Add-On

Dryer

Ozone Safe Check Valve

Air Pump

The sequence in which the sub-micronic and the molecular absorption canisters are placed, is sometimes subject to a lot of debate. Some prefer to place the sub-micronic last. You decide.

This set-up has worked for me better than what I had anticipated, and I, therefore, endorse it completely. The effluent water is of superior quality, at minimal cost, and easy installation. What else need I say.

The companies that have contributed advertising for this book
make products that are of excellent quality. If they did
not, I would not have approached them. In fact,
I use many of their products myself.
Their contribution has made it possible
to bring you this book for the $ 15.00
suggested retail that you have paid

Thiel•Aqua•Tech, my own company has contributed as well
Give your support to the american companies that bring
you truly excellent products for the Reef Aquarium

Share information with your Fellow Hobbyist, that's what the hobby is all about

Call (203) 368 2111
any time you wish, I am available to talk to you and share
my own knowledge with you.

Do not misinterpret the fact that we carry ads
in this book. The companies selected make
products that I really believe in, and find to
be of benefit to the Reef Hobby. We could have
carried many more pages of ads if we wanted to.

We hope you appreciate and understand the intent.

Albert J. Thiel
Author of this book,
The Marine Fish and Invert Reef,
Advanced Reef Keeping I,
Advanced Reef Keeping II (Dec.1989).
Editor of Marine Reef, the newsletter.

3. Water Additives, Salt :

It is important, as we have seen, to use the right type of water to start the aquarium, top-off to compensate for evaporation, and make water changes. It is also very important that after the tank is up and running, that the additives that are needed are added, and that the right kind of salt is used to prepare the water for the Reef tank.

If we are going to dispense with fancy equipment, and we are, then let's at least make sure that we cover all other required steps, to improve the water quality, and do so with the best products we can get. Don't economize in the wrong areas ! If you try to, you will be making the wrong decisions, and your aquarium and your animals will suffer.

✓ Reef Aquarium Salt :

You will be using salt for as long as you keep your tank, and salt can make up a large portion of the money you will need to spend on the aquarium. This leads many Hobbyists to buy the cheapest salt available. That is, in my opinion, a real big mistake.

Scuba divers amongst you will easily understand the following analogy : when you refill your air tanks, you want the best and cleanest "air" you can get. Your life depends on it, does'nt it ? Your corals and fish feel the same about the water and the salt you use. **Their** life depends on it. So use the best quality you can get; your tank will look better, and you will have far less problems. It would cost you much more to replace fish and invertebrates, than what you can save on salt and additives.

Fish-only tank salt is of excellent quality, but may contain impurities that you do not want in your "Reef" tank. I am especially talking about nitrates and phosphates . I cannot give evaluations of individual salts in a book, as I am sure you realize. I can, however, give you a test that you can use to determine whether or not the salt you are now using, or are planning to use, fits the quality picture I just indicated :

- mix up a batch of water with that salt,
- let the mixture stand for a few hours,
- stir once in a while, or run an airstone in the mixture,
- test for nitrates and phosphates,
- if you find any of either, try a different salt.

If you find that the salt you are now using, or plan to use, contains impurities such as nitrate and phosphate, my recommendation is that you try another salt. Why add compounds that you will have to go to great length to remove ? I ask you, why ? Especially since removing them can be quite difficult and an expensive proposition on top of it.

For obvious reasons we use Tech•Reef•Salt, an ultra pure mixture of all the elements needed, and trace elements required. You may wish to alternate its use with another less expensive salt. I personally like Hawaiian Marine Mix a lot, but there are other fine salts that fit the picture as well.

Alternatively, use a mixture that you make up yourself, of Tech Salt and another salt, in a certain proportion. For example, a mix of 25 (resp. 33) percent of one and 75 (resp. 67) percent of another one, is an excellent solution, will improve the overall quality, and will not cost a lot more than what you are doing now.

Mix the salt and the water several hours before you plan to use it. This will allow the mixture to stabilize itself, and all the components of the salt to dissolve properly. In this fashion your redox potential will also not be affected as much when you change water. Indeed, raw water (just prepared) can alter your redox potential easily by more than 100 millivolt. I have seen it happen many times. If you prepare the new water beforehand, and let the solution sit for a few hours, while aerating it, the effect will not be as drastic.

If you would like to try Tech•Reef•Salt, send us a check for fifteen dollars, including freight and handling, before Sep. 30, 1990 and a note asking for a small sample, enough for a 10 gallon water preparation, and we will gladly send it to you. This is genuinely a special salt, made to the highest specifications I can expect a manufacturer to hold himself to in making a product for us. No phone orders please. No cash on delivery either. Only by mail. Valid only in Continental United States.

✓ Trace Elements :

There are many theories about adding trace elements. Some say that the amount contained in the salts you use is plenty, and that you therefore do not need to supplement. That does not make much sense to me. Skimmers, ozonizers, and the lifeforms in the tank, continuously remove trace elements, especially the algae, both micro and macro.

Moreover, trace elements are removed in unequal amounts. Some disappear faster from the water than others. Which ones are depleted more, depends on many factors, including what type of macro-algae you grow, and what type of invertebrates you keep. Peter Wilkens, the well known German author has written extensively about this, even to the point where his experimental findings totally contradict what some avant garde German manufacturers say.

It makes a lot of sense, therefore, to use an additive to replenish such trace elements from time to time. More frequently if you skim heavily, e.g. when using the newer Venturi valve operated foam fractionators, or efficient columnar ones, operated with ozone.

How much of an additive you should use depends on the type of additive you have bought. Follow the directions of the manufacturer in this respect. Be aware, too, that most of their recommendations are on the conservative side.

Because there are no "tests" available for trace elements, no one can actually check their levels. The recommendations made are, therefore, based on personal experiences and the experience of other well known Hobbyists and researchers.

Moe (1989) expounds on the subject in The Marine Aquarium Reference, his new book, referred to several times already. Wilkens, known to most of you, is pretty clear about having to add elements to his tanks, to maintain invertebrates and corals alive and in vibrant condition. Many others before me have said so too. This is not something new, it has been around for a long time, just not highlighted often enough.

All the recommendations made in this book, and others I have written, are not meant to make you spend more money yet, but are truly meant to allow you to keep a Reef tank that will give you pleasure, and where your investment in animal life remains alive for long periods of time. Much longer than what many of you have been accustomed to, especially since we are running a basic system.

The cost of a few good additives, this one and others mentioned later, is far less, than continuously having to buy new anemones, elegance corals, sunflower corals, etc. Replacing animals and fish can get very very expensive. Do a little preventative investing, and you will fare a lot better in the long run. And besides, you will do a little too to preserve the reefs, and reduce collecting of the animals you like to keep.

✓ Vitamins :

If you were able to duplicate the food chain that exists around the Reef, you would obviously not need any additives whatsoever, including vitamins. You and I know that we cannot do that, yet, anyway.

Vitamins are an important constituent of the foods that corals and invertebrates live off around real reefs. Different lifeforms have different requirements, not all of them well-known in fact. Many have been identified, many are still not documented, or only partially so.

Mixtures of vitamins, amino acids, micro-nutrients, pigments, organic elements, and other compounds that are part of a normal food chain, are marketed. I suggest that you use them. Add them directly to the tank, or better perhaps, mix them with the food before you actually add the food to the reef aquarium. This is especially so if you use a good foam fractionator and an ozonizer. And many of you are.

There are several brands that are widely available nationwide and in Canada. Vita•Trace, Coralife and Vita-Chem are but the better known ones.

Be careful not to add too many vitamins at once if you use a protein skimmer. Some brands make the protein foam fractionator skim more strongly. As with any additive, add it regularly, in small amounts. Best is to add it by means of a drip system, in diluted form, or by means of a dosing pump. Thiel (1989) describes this in detail in Advanced Reef

Keeping Made Simple (I), and also in The Marine Fish and Invert Reef Aquarium, his other book, all published by Aardvark Press.

Many foods already contain additional vitamins. Such is the case of, for example, the Coralife line of foods, Reef Smack Melange, my own company's dry food, and others as well. Does this allow you not to use vitamin supplements ? That is a very hard question to answer, indeed. My suggestion is that you use both food and vitamins made by the same manufacturer, and then follow the directions they provide. Again, and I know I am repeating myself, protein skimmers and ozone remove many elements from the water, including vitamins.

Does it pay to change vitamin brand from time to time ? No conclusive data on such switches are available as far as I can tell, and I have, personally, not been able to notice any difference in my own tanks when doing so. Get a good brand and stick with it. Use it regularly, and increase the recommended dosage somewhat if you are strongly ozonizing. You can not overdose any way. Look for brands that contain a wide range of all known vitamins. Buy only products that look fresh when you get them, and smell like vitamins. Stick with established brands, since they have been around for a few years, they obviously must be doing something right !

✓ Special Additives :

A number of specialty additives are available. These include : Iodine, KSM, and Liquid Gold, all from my own company, and a number of nutrient formulas from Coralife, e.g. Appetite stimulant, Micro nutrients and Calcium supplement. I know of no other two companies offering such a wide assortment of specialized supplements, other than trace elements and bio-elements.

Are they necessary ? Well, if they were not, I would not have developed them, and I would not have spent money on the research necessary to do so. Additinally selling merchandise that is not "necessary" does not reflect well on a company's image, and products that are of no value to the Hobbyist would not be around for long, as no one would buy them for any length of time. Hopefully that answers your questions.

The same reasoning applies to products from companies such

as, for example, Coralife. Why would they stake their reputation and money to bring you products that are of no value ? Obviously they would not. It would be totally uneconomical to do so !

So yes, such additives are important, but not for every one. It all depends what kind of corals and invertebrates you keep, and whether or not you have a full-fledged reef tank or not. If you do, I strongly suggest that you consider using them. Again, the cost of adding a few drops of a supplement from time to time, may save you lots of dollars in the long run, not to speak of having a healthier and better looking tank, and keeping the lifeforms you have now in your aquarium alive for much longer, and growing.

A Reef tank is an aquarium where the orientation is towards corals, anemones, polyps of many kinds, mushrooms, and such type of lifeforms, supplemented, of course, with fish. The main thrust is invertebrates. A tank with many fish and 2 or 3 anemones will obviously not have the same requirements.

Iodine is a compound that is required by many higher algae, and by many invertebrates. Foam fractionation removes Iodine quickly from the water, and it needs to be replaced as a result. P. Wilkens, G. Hueckstedt, and others pointed this out years ago. Moe (1989) recently reintroduced the concept in his new book. Use Iodine supplements with care. Iodine is a strongly redox potential increasing compound. Follow the directions carefully. But use it, it is a very beneficial additive.

KSM is an additive I developed for my own use in keeping hard corals, especially Elegance. Often these corals literally come out of their hard skeleton. Hueckstedt, many years ago, hinted at a lack of certain trace elements, and P. Wilkens tested until he had evidence that the missing elements were strontium and molybdenum. KSM provides both in an easy to use mixture.

Use it if you keep Catalaphylia plicata (jardinei), better known as Elegance Corals, Gonoporia species corals, also known under names such as Sunflower, Moon, Flower Pot corals (and others still), Euphyllia corals or plate corals, and other types of hard skeleton corals. If you only keep anemones, tube worms, mushroom corals (Actinodiscus sp.), and corals without a hard skeleton, you do not need KSM. If you fall in the other category, do yourself a favor, and invest in a few ounces every month or so. Don't buy large quantities, you only need ounces.

Micro-Nutrients are a definite requirement in every Reef. Since they are the ones present in the smallest quantities, they are also the first ones to be depleted. Will you see your Corals perk up when you use them ? Probably not, but you will find that in the long run your Reef will do much better if you do use them. I do. The product is hard to manufacture, and the only company at the time of this writing who had it available was Coralife, which of course also markets many other Reef specific products.

Liquid Gold : this is a very special additive, and one that is very close to me. I developed it over the last 5 years, and finalised its formula about 1 year ago. I use it every day, and would not do without it. I call it by that catchy name because I really believe that it does special things for the animals in my Reef set-ups.

"Liquid Gold" contains not only nutrients, and can therefore be considered a food, but it also contains selective amounts of trace elements, small amounts of 4 vitamins that I consider very important for corals and invertebrates, free amino acids, fatty acids, pigments, a selected number of organic compounds necessary to filter feeders and corals of amongst other the Actinodiscus types, iodine, strontium, molybdenum, carbodydrate, saccharides, polysaccharides, organic forms of metals such as gold, iron and silver, and many many others yet. It is truly a super-mixture of "all" the elements and compounds, organic and inorganic, that available literature has demonstrated to be both necessary and beneficial for corals, invertebrates and other lifeforms kept in Reef Aquariums. I unequivocally, and without hesitation, highly recommend it to you too.

You do not need much of it, so don't be alarmed by its price. I could, of course, sell it in diluted form, make you use more of it, and charge less per container. You would then go through more containers. The end result, cost-wise, would still be the same. It is, therefore, sold in 2 oz dropper bottles that are easy to use, and in 4 oz refills.

Appetite Stimulant from Coralife is another additive that is "special", insomuch as they are the only ones making such a product.

Use it according to their instructions and you will be impressed with the results you obtain. Feeding is triggered by certain stimuli, and that is exactly what this product does. It promotes feeding.

Ridalgex : a water additive by Thiel•Aqua•Tech for those Hobbyists who have difficulty with their water chemistry, and who, as a result, experience high amounts of micro-algae and slime algae growth in their tanks. Although better water chemistry would take care of the problem, when such is not practical or not possible, Ridalgex will rid the tank of undesirable slime, hair and other micro-algae. It increases the time between cleaning the glass (or acrylic) as well. Safe for reef tanks, and effective. Sold in 1 ounce dropper bottles. This is a product to be used when needed, e.g. when normal procedures do not rid the aquarium of red, slime, brownish and other type of algae.

Micro-Algae Control : a product similar to the one just mentioned above, to control the growth of all forms of micro-algae, including slime, hair, and others, on rocks, glass, and in the aquarium. This is one is by Coralife, a very reputable company that brings you many other Reef and Salt water tank products. Safe for reef tanks, and very effective. Sold in Coralife's usual large bottles wtih dropper top. This product, based on the instructions, is geared towards maintenance and prevention.

KH Generator Fluid : any tank containing hard corals needs to be run at a relatively high carbonate hardness. Thiel (1989) explains the reasons for this in detail in both his books on Reef Tanks : The Marine Fish and Invert Reef, and Advanced Reef Keeping Made Simple (I). Many other authors concur.

Suggested levels are between 12 and 18 dKH, or between 4.28 and 6.43 meq/liter. This is much higher than the carbonate hardness one gets from using aquarium salts, obviating the need for a supplement. Peter Wilkens (1973) suggest levels that are even higher : dKH 15 to 20. Wilkens (1973) and Thiel (1989) both suggest the addition of "kalkwasser" or limewater, over and above the use of carbonate and bicarbonate additives. More references on how to do this exactly, can be found in "Marine Reef" the newsletter.

Tablets, and powders, are available from several manufacturers, e.g. Instant Ocean (Aquarium Systems). Fluids are available from

Thiel•Aqua•Tech and from Coralife as well. You can even make your own buffers if you take the time to do so, and can get the chemicals needed. Moe (1989) gives a suggested, and totally safe, formula based on the use of sodium ash and sodium bi-carbonate, a two component mixture.

The reason I recommend liquids, and have been doing so for years, rather than tablets, is that the latter may make your skimmer foam excessively, resulting in floods. Liquids do not need to contain binders, and can therefore be added safely, without having to worry about your protein skimmer.

Be aware, too, that some manufacturers try to sell you straight baking soda (sodium bicarbonate) for a hefty price. Although that is obviously one of the necessary constituents of a good KH generator, it is only one of at least 4 compounds that should be present. Don't pay premium prices for a product that is not complete, even if it comes in a nice container, has an appealing color, and may come from abroad. You can buy pure baking soda for pennies at your local supermarket, and it will not even contain binders that make your skimmer foam excessively, as some of the products referred to above do.

As a general remark : Colored products are not necesarily "better", indeed, color is often a harmless dye that is added, and that dye does not enhance the efficiency of the product, it just makes it look better. Granted, the dyes used that we looked at, are safe.

A good KH generator should not only raise your carbonate hardness, but it should keep it there for quite some time. How long, is hard to state because it depends on the biological load of the tank. The higher that biological load, the more organic and other acidity will be present, and the faster the carbonate hardness will drop. Carbonate hardness is also a factor of how many algae, both micro and macro, are growing in the tank. Algae require carbon dioxide because of the carbon present in it.

If they cannot find free carbon dioxide, or if they cannot find enough free CO_2, they remove the carbon from the the bi-carbonates and carbonates present in the water. At the extreme, biogenic decalcification takes place, and a white powdery dust covers the rocks and the glass. This, of course, reduces the carbonate hardness greatly. Even without biogenic decalcification, carbonate hardness is reduced and needs to be adjusted by the addition of an additive. Adding CO_2 to the tank, does not do away with the need to adjust the KH, to the contrary, it may increase it (Thiel, 1988). This is described in detail in "The Marine Fish and Invert Reef Aquarium" and also in some issues of Marine Reef, Aardvark Press' newsletter, of which bound issues are available as well.

$KMnO_4$: Hobbyists who do not use ozone, and some who do, but have a need for more oxidative power in the water, use a strongly diluted solution of Potassium permanganate, and add it drop-wise to the tank or filter sump (best).

The use of oxidizers on a more generalized basis, is a rather recent occurance, and needs careful watching. Several German sources I deal with find it very helpful, providing the user has the maturity necessary to deal with a chemical where the difference between the right dose, and too much, is not all that large.

$KMnO_4$ is a strong oxidizer and not a chemical you want to play around with, unless you know exactly what you are doing. It can, as far as I have been able to determine, be added safely to an aquarium, for brief periods of time, and intermittently. If you are new to this type of a chemical compound, best is to use the liquid form.

What is important, is that you buy the product from a company that you can rely on to have tested the strength of the solution they sell. It should never in my opinion, exceed 550 millivolt of ORP (redox), and should be added to your tank only in the slow drip method fashion. If the product is too strong, after you test it with your own redox meter, further dilutions are necessary, and must be done by using distilled (U.S.P. purified) water only. In fact, water purer than USP purified would be even better. Unless you are really familiar with how this works, do not use $KMnO_4$ until someone who does has carefully explainedto you how to go about adding it.

Hydrogen Peroxide : an absolute no for reef tanks. It can quickly raise the oxygen content of the water, but it can also do so much damage so quickly, that we ask you to not use it at all. Wilkens and Hueckstedt have both described methods of adding it safely. Experience shows, however, that hobbyists usually overdose, and that all corals and invertebrates greatly suffer, to the point where they will be lost.

If you must use hydrogen peroxide, you should do so only after you have consulted with someone who has done so before you, and has experience with strengths and dosages. I know of no product in the hobby using hydrogen peroxide safely as an additive.

Sodium perborate : same remarks as for hydrogen peroxide. Please do not use this chemical either. It works fine in fish-only tanks, just as peroxide does, but in Reef aquariums too many disastrous situations have been reported by hobbyists who did not really heed the instructions. One can even find mixtures of the above two chemicals. Stay away from those too. The latter are usually sold as products that will quickly increase the amount of dissolved oxygen in the water.

Kalkwasser : touched upon briefly early in this chapter, kalkwasser is a mixture that is used to increase not the "carbonate" hardness of the water, but the "calcium" hardness.

It is a very important additive for every hobbyist who maintains hard corals, as the latter use the elements in the kalkwasser to grow and multiply. The type of corals referred to include, for example, Meat coral, Sunflower coral, Elegance coral, Bubble coral, and similar ones. All coralline algae benefit from the addition of kalkwasser as well, of course.

Kalkwasser, or Limewater, has been advocated for invertebrate and coral aquariums since the days of Guido Hueckstedt and Peter Wilkens, in the 60's and 70's, in Germany, but nobody seems to have given it the importance it deserves, when the Reef Aquarium became a fact in the United States and Canada.

George Smit's constant reference to the need for having layers of "calcite" in the water, under the trickle filter, may have been the closest to suggesting that calcium carbonate, and calcium as such, are important in a Reef Aquarium. He did not go as far, however, as to suggest the addition of some form of calcium compound in a dissolved manner.

Adding Kalkwasser is, in my opinion, just as important as adding salt, or maintaing the right pH, temperature, etc. It is certainly as important as adding the right kind of supplements, e.g. Iodine, KSM, and others described in this chapter.

At Thiel•Aqua•Tech we add it every day, and have done so for years, with very positive results for all the corals we keep, and we keep many types. My company, therefore, also sells it to the discerning Hobbyist. We use USP grade calcium hydroxide and triple distilled water in its preparation, and run lab grade carbon dioxide through it, to adjust the pH. Marine Reef, our newsletter, recently carried an article describing how you can prepare it yourself. It is not easy, but it can be done, as long as you have a source for the chemicals, and already use carbon dioxide on your system.

X-Nitrate : a granular compound sold in several sizes that is placed somewhere in the water flow to remove nitrates, and some phosphates, in an aerobic manner. Aerobically means that this product does so in the presence of oxygen. It is, therefore, much easier to use than the so-called "denitrators" that are available, and that work on the semi anaerobic principle (facultatively aerobic-anaerobic bacteria), with the addition of a carbon source (the nutrient).

X-nitrate is a natural compound, must be rinsed well before it is used, and cannot be regenerated once it has exhausted its absorption ability. It is not a zeolite. For Hobbyists whose tanks contain high amounts of nitrate, for whatever reason, this product is a very welcome addition to the reef product array. You can, for instance, test for nitrates with the Route 4 Marine Technology low range nitrate test . This will give you a good indication as to when you should replace the product. Incidentally, that same company markets a full range of Reef water tests.

Nitrate-Phosphate Control : Coralife also markets a product that removes nitrate and phosphate from the water. Again the compound must be placed in the water flow. As the water contacts the product, the latter removes nitrates and phosphates.

Low nitrates and low phosphates are important in reef aquariums, because their levels affect the appearance of the invertebrates that you keep, and also affect the amount and type of micro-algae that will grow in the aquarium. Levels that are too high make the tank look dull and not appealling at all.

ON TRICKLE FILTERS

TRATION TECHNOLOGY

IN TRICKLE FILTRATION

BBYIST WHO WANTS

LY THE BEST

R, COMPACT, AND SELF CONTAINED

OM THIEL·AQUA·TECH

OF COURSE...

IN THE UNITED STATES

• Conclusion :

We reviewed most of the additives that you should use on your reef aquarium. There are probably still others, and newer ones may have appeared by the time your read this book.

Refer to an authoritative source of information to keep yourself up-to-date on the latest developments in Reef Aquarium keeping, the most challenging part of the marine hobby, but also the one where water quality is the most important, in terms of the type of success that you can expect.

Moreover, because the Hobby is still so "young" in this country, a lot of misinformation is unfortunately circulated, not willingly, of course, but because many shops and hobbyists have little experience that can be backed up with notes, time, empyric evidence, etc.

There are several excellent magazines dedicated to the hobby. Some are more orientated to marine environments than others. We highly recommend Freshwater and Marine Aquarium, better known to some as FAMA, and, of course, there is our own newsletter : Marine Reef, that deals with nothing but reef aquarium technology and the animals that you can, or may already be, keeping in your tank.

It is now in its second year of publication, and all issues of the first year, numbered 1 through 17, are available in soft bound form. Call Aardvark Press for details if you are interested. Signed, numbered, hardbound editions are available as well.

4. Lighting for the Reef Tank

■ Introduction :

If there still is a controversial subject in Reef Keeping, this is it. Thousands upon thousands of words have been written, recommending just about every type of light that is possibly available on the market. This includes most types of fluorescent fixtures and tube combinations, and many other forms of lighting, especially high intensity discharge ones, as well as a whole number of hybrid systems.

I certainly do not have all the answers here either, but I do know what has worked for me for many years, ever since I first saw metal halide lights, in Germany, over Reef aquariums in Pet shops and at Hobbyist's homes, over their reef aquariums.

Their tanks looked so much better than what I was accustomed to see that, when I represented a German company in this country, I was most enthused about bringing that type of lighting into the market place in the United States and Canada. I experimented with these metal halides (Osram Power Stars at that time), and had the same type of success over my own aquariums as the tanks that I had seen overseas, in Germany, France and England.

Soon thereafter, a foresighted American manufacturer, Omer Dersom of Energy Savers Unlimited, took a large commercial risk, and decided to offer metal halide lighting to the Hobbyist at much more affordable prices than what they had been available for up to then. First he introduced 4300 K degree bulbs, and recently 5500 K degree Daylight (blue-white) ones. His strategy obviously worked, and such metal halides are now the norm of every discriminating Hobbyist I know.

Still, some re-sellers in this country advocate a different form of lighting, and put much too great an importance, I feel, on the use of actinic lights, often, if not always, mixed with other fluorecent tubes. To me, there is no question at all, that time will prove me right. Metal halide lighting is the only safe way to go, and where you should put your money if you are in the market for lighting for a Reef tank.

Do not misunderstand me, even though you can keep quite nice reef aquariums with certain types of fluorecent lights, providing you use enough of them; the difference between such tanks, and similar tanks run with metal halide lights, is like day and night. If fluorecent tubes is what you use now, see later in this chapter for suggestions on how to improve your existing set up, by either changing the bulbs, or increasing respectively their numbers and/or output.

That metal halide lighting is the only way to go, is quite a strong statement, but one that I believe to be absolutely correct. My own experience, and that of many hobbyists I know, is plenty of evidence to support that statement. Tanks lighted with metal halides, especially the daylight types (5500K), just do a great deal better than other tanks I have seen. You can find evidence of that in my new series of videotapes dealing with " The Reef Aquarium Corals and Inverts : Types and Care" Parts 1 to 3, available from Aardvark Press.

Aquariums lighted with fluorecent tubes, just do not allow the corals and invertebrates to develop the way they do in tanks lighted with metal halides, and high Kelvin degree mercury vapors (clear types). The tanks may look nice, and some hard corals and some mushroom corals may show vivid colors, but at the sacrifice of their physical size and appearance. To me, at least, that is not an acceptable trade-off.

The only caveat when using metal halide lighting, is that you must use the right kind of metal halide bulb. If you do not, you will not get the results that I can otherwise guarantee you. The halides must be of the "high intensity discharge" type, meaning you will need a transformer box with them.

Don't be afraid though, when you buy such a lighting set-up you obtain all the parts needed in one purchase. You will not have to go out and buy any other parts separately. Keep this remark in mind, indeed, if you are offered a so-called metal halide that does not require a ballast (transformer) and that you plug directly into the wall outlet, you are being offered the wrong light ! Those are mostly Tungsten halogen quartz lights, which give off a lot of light, but also very yellow light, not suitable for the reef tank.

■ Metal Halide Lighting and Corals :

Ever since I wrote "The Marine Fish and Invert Reef Aquarium" book, hundreds and hundreds of Hobbyists have called to ask questions about lighting, and also why I am so adamant about using metal halide bulbs. The reason is very simple: because they allow me to keep a Reef tank with invertebrates that open to the fullest I have ever seen, and keep them that way for the longest of times, not just a few days or weeks. Anyone who has seen my main show tanks can attest to that.

Visualize purple mushrooms (Actinodiscus sp. and Actinodiscus sharonii) that are about 1/4 inch when they are closed, open to about 3 1/2 to 4 inches when fully open under metal halide 5500 K Coralife™ bulbs.

Visualize the same purple Actinodiscus species mushrooms lift off the rocks on which they are, so you can see a stem underneath them of about 3/8 to 1/2 an inch in diameter, and well over an inch long. I have never seen that happen in a tank with fluorescent tubes to a degree that frequent as it happens in aquariums with MH 5500K bulbs. The size coloring, and shape of Actinodiscus sharonii is only one example of what can be achieved with such bulbs over a Reef aquarium.

Another good example of what metal halides can do for corals, is the coral Catalaphyllia jardinei, sometimes refered to as plicata as well (common names Elegance, or Elegant). Although they may stretch to quite a large size under strong fluorescent lighting, you will see them "grow" to about 1.5 to 2 times that size under metal halide lighting, combined, of course, with good water quality (redox of 300 mv or more in the aquarium itself). Some specimens in my tank are literaly huge, especially considering that the hard part underneath in only about 5 inches long and 3/4 of an inch wide, and is not branched.

Elephant ear corals, Discosoma types, which normally stay flat and close to the rock to which they are attached, open up wide, stretch and curl at the edges, even when they are not feeding, and become larger than you have ever seen them under fluorscent lighting, even when supplemented with special blue and green bulbs. Elephant ear corals are delicate corals, feeding on both live foods and extracting nutrients from the water and from photosynthesis.

Many anemones, e.g. Clownfish anemones, of the "ritteri" type, migrate upwards closer to the metal halide lights, proof, obviously, that they find it beneficial. Additionally, the ones we have in the home show tank, do not lose their colors. I keep 2 large ones, and both are a good 15 inches accross when they open up completely a few hours after the lights have been on. The noteworthy fact, of course, is that they were only about half that size when I originally placed them in that tank.

Euphyllia ancora, the coral with the kidney shaped end of tentacles (as opposed to the Tee-shaped end of hammer head corals, Euphyllia cristata), stretches its tentacles to a length of possibly as much as 6 inches. In the same tank Euphyllia glabrescens, the coral with the whitish round ended tentacles increases in shape to be point where it bulges out of the hard skeleton.

I could go on and on, but I am sure that you have gotten the point I am trying to make. Although other forms of lighting may be adequate, metal halides, of the high intensity discharge type, 5500 K, give better results in Reef Tanks.

It has also been said that metal halides "burn" corals ! That erroneous rumor is now heard many times in discussions about light between Hobbyists ! Be aware that some companies that we think were responsible for that statement, now sell metal halides imported from another country, whereas before they were touting, over and over again, the benefits of actinic light.

Metal halide lights, used properly, with UV shields, if so recommended, do not harm corals. Not a bit. The sun gives off much more UV than even the strongest metal halides can, and beats on the coral reef day in, and day out, granted with the water as a partial shield.

Actinic light can under certain circumstances be beneficial, especially if the other lights used in conjunction with it, are not of as full a spectrum as they should. In this respect be aware that Osram bulbs, as now sold in this country, have a spectrum of only 4300 K, not nearly as good, for our purpose, as the newer 5500 K metal halides. 4300 Kelvin degrees is very good, but 5500 K is much better. The experiences of others who have used them, and my own, are proof of that.

Actinic light will, often, give the tank an eerie look, especially if you use several strong ones. This distorts the appearance of colors, and makes animals look unnatural. Metal halides, because they are a much more "complete" light source, do not. In fact, the 5500 K proprietary Coralife bulb, is rated as a daylight bulb, meaning that you will perceive the colors of the animals in your tank as "true" colors. On paper that may sound unimportant, but in reality, looking at an aquarium that does not look "real" is very strange for anyone visiting your house.

The photograph on the cover of this book was taken around 3:00 pm, while 700 watt of metal halide lights of the 5500 K type were burning for several hours. Those purple mushrooms look a lot better, I feel, than some others I have seen in photographs.

How much light intensity should you install? A lot if you can. The minimum I recommend is 2.5 watt per gallon of water in your tank. More if you want better results. Over a 55 gallon tank you can easily place 175 watts or more of metal halide lighting. I have 700 watts over a 135 in my house, and all are 5500 K metal halide bulbs.

Availability of lights, and their respective wattage, may make it necessary for you to adjust somewhat upward or somewhat downwards, but use 2.5 to 5 watt per gallon as a guideline.

You can, nowadays, buy metal halides mounted in hoods (Coralife-Energy Savers), or as pendants (Thiel•Aqua•Tech). Which one of these types to prefer is a totally personal choice.

Both types are equally effective at providing the right light for your corals and invertebrates. Hoods are closer to the water, and may thus be more efficient than pendants; pendants on the other hand leave the top of the tank open, and appear more attractive to some. There are many similar trivial differences of that type between both and, as a result, there are proponents and opponents of both types. Fortunately both types are available for sale in both the United States and Canada, and so the choice is yours.

If the light intensity you require, or plan to use, is lower than 175 watt, no 5500 K bulbs are available at this time. You can of course still use such a bulb, but in pendant form. This will allow you to place it a distance from the water, thus reducing the intensity, and spreading the light out better over the entire aquarium. Alternatively you should use 4300 K bulbs, which are available in 100 and 175 watts versions.

Contrary to popular belief, based on some articles that appeared in hobby magazines, metal halide light gives off a lot of "blue" light as well, especially the newer 5500 Kelvin degree Coralife bulbs.

Cost is always a factor, unfortunately. Metal halide lights can be expensive, especially if you need several of them. Buying pendants can be a significant expense, albeit a good one.

Fortunately, Energy Savers Coralife came to the rescue some time ago by offering, what they refer to as, **The Light Spot**, a sort of do-it-yourself metal halide lighting set-up, greatly reducing the cost of installing metal halides over your aquarium. For more information call them direct, they advertise in all hobby magazines. We tried one, and can attest to the fact that their installation is really very simple, and the price is right too...

■ Fluorescent Lighting

Many Hobbyists now use fluorescent tubes over their tanks. At Thiel•Aqua•Tech we have used both metal halide lighting and fluorescent tubes too. We have, as you may have surmized, found that over reef aquariums metal halide lights give much better results, and have switched to using only the latter type. We also described the results earlier.

If you are now using fluorescent tubes, or are considering doing so, our recommendations are as follows :

- use daylight tubes (5000 to 5500 kelvin degrees)
- use as many as you can place over the tank
- use only one actinic if you absolutely feel you must

- only run the actinic for a few hours a day
- follow the guidelines given earlier with regard to intensity
- change the bulbs about every 7 to 8 months.
- run your lights for at least 12 hours a day.
- if the bulbs you are now using are older than 6 months, definitely change them, and install new daylight ones.

Because it often is difficult, if not impossible, to get enough regular fluorescent tubes (400mA) over the aquarium to match the minimum of 2.5 watt per gallon recommended, one solution that many Hobbyists resort to, is to use high output (800mA) fluorescent tubes. Such bulbs give more intensity per watt, and can be a viable solution, albeit not necessarily a less expensive one than using metal halides.

Check with Energy Savers, as that company offers a wide variety of hoods, in many configurations, and may be able to come up with a workable solution for you. You could, for example, get the hood from them, and acquire bulbs elsewhere, if that is the way you decide to go.

Besides regular and high output fluorescent tubes, some specialty lights are available as well. Usually these lights are of the daylight or higher spectrum, and are worth considering too. We do not recommend very high output (1200mA) tubes, because they lose their spectrum very quickly, and would need replacing every 3 months or so, making their use a very expensive way to go.

Because new types of lighting appear on the market all the time, watching for new developments in this area is certainly something a Reef Hobbyist should do. As techniques evolve, and progress is made, one can be sure that leading lighting companies such as Energy Savers, for example, will bring you what is state-of-the-art as time goes on. Progress is what makes this hobby exciting, challenging and moving forward to bring us even better reef aquariums.

At this stage of affairs in the Reef hobby, the best that is available, in my experience, are the daylight metal halides made by Coralife. I highly recommend them, and use them myself with great success. Their price is also less than a third of the 4300 K Osram bulbs advocated by some German circles.

5. Maintenance - Husbandry

Regardless of how well you set your aquarium up, regardless of the expense you go to equipment-wize, if you do not maintain both the aquarium, and service the equipment, problems are in store for you. Even the best of equipment needs to be serviced from time to time; the best pumps money can buy need cleaning from time to time; the best filter around needs cleaning out too, etc.

Husbandry and maintenance are really two different tasks. Maintenance is taking care of your tank's equipment. Husbandry is caring for the tank itself, i.e. the water changes, cleaning the substrate, removing detritus, taking out dead or dying algae, adding water to compensate for evaporation, dispensing water additives, testing the water quality at regular intervals, and tasks of that nature. Both are very distinct of each other.

Maintenance is necessary mostly to prevent either :
• equipment failure
• equipment malfunction
• erroneous readings if you use meters to monitor certain water conditions
• problems with equipment that can directly and quickly influence the water quality, which in turn affects the lifeforms.

Husbandry are all those tasks that ensure that once the water quality is good, that it remains there, and that your tank always looks at its best. Husbandry requires more work, and certainly more dedication. In highly automated systems a lot of these tasks can be automated and do not have to be performed by the tank's owner. In our small Reef, the one discussed in this book, this is not the case. You, the Hobbyist will have to perform the work, and you will have to do so on a regular basis, not just once in a while, when you think about it, or when it is convenient.

Successful tanks, especially reef tanks, cannot be kept if they are not cared for as they need to be. Let's face it, the best of cars needs maintenance and care too; the best of golf clubs need to be properly taken care of; the best of SCUBA gear needs constant attention to keep it in top shape. Well, the same applies to your reef tank, and even more so, because you are dealing with live animals and invertebrates.

The quality of the water in which they live is as important to them, as the air you breathe is to you. Even more so, because they, the lifeforms in the tank, cannot do anything about it. They have to rely on you, the owner of the aquarium.

If all those reasons are not enough yet to convince you, think of all the money you have invested in a reef system, and in the rocks and lifeforms that are in it. Replacing livestock that died because you did not take proper care of the tank, can be very expensive, but is something you can control, something you can avoid. All you have to do is "care" for the hobby you got into. Tanks do not take care of themselves...

I have outlined, in great detail, a schedule for reef tank maintenance in my book : The Marine Fish and Invert Reef Aquarium, one geared to more automated systems. Disregard the items that do not apply to you, and take care of the others. If you do not have the book it is available from stores nationwide, or from us directly.

What I am more concerned with here, in Small Reef Aquarium Basics, is husbandry, not because maintenance is not important, it is, but because little is written about husbandry in magazines and other books that deal with Reef tanks (of course there are'nt that many available to begin with).

Let's review some of the tasks that I consider important, and that I perform myself on my home aquarium, and on the tanks we keep at the business :

Cleaning :
Cleaning includes several areas of concern. A very important one is the tank bottom : you should remove any dead material, uneaten food, organic detritus, dead algae, etc. as soon as you see it. Do not let it decompose, all such achieves is fouling the water up by producing

breakdown products that increase the load on the biological filters, by producing ammonia, and subsequently nitrite, and nitrate, not to speak of other by-products, phosphates, both organic and inorganic being just two of them.

Of course, dead fish, or dead invertebrates, however small they may be, should be taken out at once. All that you would achieve by not doing so, is letting them "rot" so to speak, and stress your filters, as well as all the lifeforms in the tank. Organic breakdown not only adds noxious compounds "to" the water, but it takes beneficial compounds, e.g. oxygen "out" of the water. That is a double-edged sword.

Often, a greyish to brownish material referred to in the hobby as mulm, collects on the bottom of the tank. Incidentally, I have not been able to find an exact definition for that word in 5 different comprehensive dictionaries I looked into, including the latest 2nd Edition of The Random House Unabridged Dictionary of the English Language, and Science and Technology dictionaries as well. Mulm is usually defined, in the hobby, as material that is totally mineralized, meaning it cannot break down further, and is, therefore, considered harmless.

The problem is how does the hobbyist know whether it is mulm or not that is lying on the bottom of the tank ? My recommendation, therefore, is that you syphon off anything that lies on the substrate, or bottom, or rocks, that is not something you yourself added to the aquarium. You might call it the better safe than sorry approach.

Most important for you is to clean all your mechanical filters at least once a week, and preferably more often. Any material trapped in the filters is still part of the system, as I explained elsewhere, the only difference is, that you do not see it anymore. Leaving it in the filters, will start decay with the resulting reduction in oxygen in the water, the appearance of ammonia, etc. You may not look at it as such, but an overflow corner filter, a syphon surface skimmer, and other such items, also trap dirt and need to be cleaned.

The bottom of the trickle filter, the drip plate, and any mechanical filtering device you may have inside the trickle filter, falls in this category as well. The same applies, of course, to micron filters, sand filters, and other such canister type arrangements.

Some Hobbyists like to clean the rocks in the tank from time to time, to remove accumulated dust and other material. That is usually best done by directing the output of a very small power head at them, and letting the dust and other material get caught in your normal mechanical filters. If you are going to do this, do it before you clean your mechanical filters. It will save you from cleaning them twice the same day, or within a day of each other. While on the subject of power heads, they have a tendency to collect dirt too, and must be cleaned as well.

It is obvious, but for the sake of being complete, the glass or acrylic of the tank must be cleaned regularly as well, including the back and sides. They may be harder to get to, but clean as much as you can. Whatever you can remove, is no longer part of the system and cannot decay, as a result.

Water Changes and Level Adjustments :

I have made recommendations on how to do this, how often, and why, elsewhere in this book already. I stress again though, that I really feel that changing water is an absolute must. Don't be fooled by advertising that claims that if you use such and such a product you no longer need to change water. In my experience such is not possible. You must make regular and small water changes. Your tank will look much better, and more vibrant.

Although not necessarily a form of cleaning, chemical filters such as Poly Filters, activated carbon, resins, etc. need to be either changed on a regular basis, or in the case of Poly Filters, rinsed and evaluated to determine whether or not they can be used for longer. If you are a firm believer in activated carbon, and rely on it as your chemical filter, change it every few weeks; depending on the load your tank carries, sooner or later. I usually recommend a maximum of 4 to 5 weeks.

Water Quality Management :

The only way for you to know how good, or bad, the water quality really is, is by testing it on a regular basis, **and keeping notes of the results in a diary**. Testing, and keeping records, is an absolute must in a basic reef aquarium, because you cannot rely on instrumentation to monitor conditions for you.

Additionally, by keeping records you will be able to build up a history of how your tank "behaves", so to speak. Any deviation in water quality parameters will then become more obvious, as you will be able to refer to previous readings of a particular item, compound, or state that you are testing for.

We suggest that you acquire the following tests :
- ammonia
- nitrite
- nitrate (low range)
- phosphate (low range)
- dissolved oxygen (in mg/l)
- residual ozone (if you are using an ozonizer)
- carbonate hardness
- iron (if you keep macro-algae and fertilize)
- pH
- and a real accurate thermometer.

There are many other tests still, such as silicate, and high range nitrate and phosphate, copper, carbon dioxide, amongst others, but I personally feel you do not need those in a basic reef tank.

Perform tests on a regular schedule, and keep notes. Some tests you may want to perform more often than others. Dissolved oxygen, pH and carbonate hardness are but three. Other tests you may only want to perform once a week. The key is however to "make" the tests and, again, keep records so you have something to look back at to determine how your tank is doing this time, versus the last time you tested. It is unreasonable to expect that you will remember what the dissolved oxygen levels, for instance, were the last time you tested.

Of course, testing has one other major advantage : you learn all there is to know about your tank. You would be surprised how helpful that will be, when someday something goes awry.

When your tank does not look good, and you need to determine what to do, to bring it back to its usual shape, you will need not only to have the tests available, but know how to interpret the results. You will also need to know where the tank is different, test-wize, when it looks out of shape. If you have no notes to refer to, such will not be possible, or to say the least, extremely hard to do. That, then, brings about more problems because you will not know how to react, because you basically do not know what to react to. Such puts you in a situation where the tank controls "you" and not vice-versa. You should never let that happen. You should be the one in control.

Time and time again I get phone calls that make it evident that the Hobbyist has no clue what any of the values that are normally measured are, or were, when the tank looked good. That makes it practically impossible for me to help them. Indeed, what do I go by, to recommend a cure ? Stating, for instance, my fish have "ich", is only the result of some tank water chemistry disorder. The problem lies elsewhere. The fish became infected with ich, because they were stressed. The key is, then, to determine where the stress came from, and to do that, one needs water quality parameters to make a diagnosis and suggestions.

There is one test that needs to be performed that has not been mentioned yet : salinity, or specific gravity. There are several ways to do so. A good hydrometer, or a salinometer, or a special salinity test (for example the one sold by Lamotte Chemicals). Most hobbyists use a hydrometer, and that is perfectly fine, as long as it is a unit that has been calibrated for aquarium use, temperature-wize. Many are calibrated for 59 degrees Fahrenheit and not 75-76, the temperature at which you normally run your tank, or should anyway. In this respect you may wish to refer to Martin Moe's first book : The Marine Aquarium Handbook, beginner to breeder, for a chart that indicates the adjustments to be made at various temperatures.

Where do you get all these tests ? Companies such as Route 4 Marine Technology, my own company, and some others, offer an array of tests. The key is to get the right ones. When, for instance, I indicated that you should get the "low range", I suggest you do. A high range test is of little value in a reef tank. You can also get tests from the companies that make them, e.g. LaMotte, Chemetrics, Ecological Labs, Hach, etc. but they usually only sell lots, not single tests, and may get more money for their tests than if you went through say, Route 4 Marine Tech, or one of their many distributors.

For each of the measurements (tests) suggested, there are, obviously ideal, acceptable, and non acceptable levels. Many authors differ in opinion on what those various numbers should be. I can give you the ones that I usually recommend, and have found to be safe. You may wish to check some other sources, if you want a second opinion.

I have found, over time, that for many parameters it is difficult to differentiate between ideal and acceptable, so I will only list one number, or a range in parts per million, or milligrams per liter :

- Ammonia   0.00 ppm
- Nitrite   0.00 to 0.1 ppm maximum
- Nitrate   1.00 ppm $N-NO_3$ maximum
- Nitrate   5.00 ppm as NO_3
- Dissolved 0_2 saturation or higher, usually >7mg/l
- Phosphate   0.1 to 0.2 ppm total PO_4
- Copper   0.00 ppm (except for traces in the salt)
- Iron   0.1 to 0.5 ppm maximum
- Residual 0_3 none detectable with O-tolidine tests
- Carbonate   Hardness of 5.35-6.45 meq/l or as some express it 15 to 18 dKH (German degrees)
- Calcium   Hardness of 60-80 ppm
- pH   8.0 to 8.3
- Spec. Grav.   1.022 to 1.025, preferably the latter
- Temperature   75 to 76 Fahrenheit
- Redox pot.   350-390 mv in the tank itself A recent article in Marine Reef gives a much more detailed review (Vol 2 Nr 22)
- Conductivity   Around 51000 to 53000 microsiemens
- TDS   total dissolved solids 460-470 ppm

Keep in mind that in your small reef tank you may not be measuring several of these, since you will not be using instruments, or at least not automation instrumentation such as "controllers". They are just given as a reference, because some Hobbyists use so-called pen-type meters.

With the risk of being accused of repeating myself, test on a regular basis, and keep notes. Add a comment or two about the animals, respectively invertebrates in the tank, how they looked, and very importantly : the time of day, and how long after feeding time that you performed these tests. Adding food will affect many tests; you should as a result not test within 4 hours of feeding. Best is to always test at the same time of day, or if you test more than once, to also match those times, as many tests are affected by the rate of metabolism of the animals.

Additives :

Water quality management includes the addition of a number of water additives, i.e. trace elements, vitamins, KSM, Iodine, and others discussed elsewhere in the book. This is an important part of good tank husbandry. You should set up a regular schedule for yourself to do so, based on the conclusions you have drawn for your tank, from the material you have read about these additives in this and other books.

Visual Inspection :

Often you just "look" at your tank. From time to time, however, you should consider this a detailed visual inspection. Not only will you learn a lot about your aquarium, i.e. what small animal life is in it, but it may pinpoint actions you have to take. For example, you may notice dead algae underneath some rocks, something you would not see if you just looked briefly at the aquarium.

Inspect your aquarium at night too, not just during the day. Again, you will notice animal life that you normally do not see during the day; you will learn how some of the animals, and invertebrates, that you keep look after the lights are out, and you may, again, find that you need to take some action, i.e. you may see bristle worms which you will have to try to remove somehow.

Taking Corrective Action :

Of course, anytime something is wrong with the tank, you will have to take corrective action to bring the tank back to its normal shape. The latter really means bringing the water chemistry back to where it should be, at least in 99 percent of the cases. What to do in each situation is not part of this book, but there are many other ones, and of course Marine Reef, our Newsletter, that give advice for many types of actions that you may need and want to undertake.

You could also call or talk to your local Pet Shop, the local Aquarium Society, or call someone whose opinion you respect, especially after you have exhausted all other avenues. Many volumes could be written about what to do when something go wrong in a reef tank, and still each situation would be unique, because each tank is different. The filtration differs, the animal population is not the same, one tank has macro-algae, another one not, some tanks have lots of invertebrates, others do not, one is well taken care of, another one not, etc.

Feeding :

Feeding is also part of good husbandry. Feeding a Reef Aquarium is however quite more complex than feeding a fish-only tank, because of the difference in the nature of the animals kept.

There are so many different manufacturers of fish foods nowadays that it is easy to get confused. One thing is clear however : I said "fish" food not reef tank food. In the reef tank food area the choice boils down to very few. Those who have taken the time to develop foods specifically designed for corals and invertebrates that need extra nutrition, besides what they can gather from the photosynthesis of their symbiotic algae, the Zooxanthellae. One such company is Coralife, which offers not only excellent liquid food varieties, but also frozen ones. I can highly recommend their foods, and use them myself in addition to the ones made by my own company (Reef Smack Melange).

Feeding is a process that is complex, insomuch as each type of animal you keep may have different requirements. This makes it necessary to feed highly complex and complete forms of food. This also makes it hard for me to recommend what, and how often, you should feed the lifeforms that you may be keeping in your tank, in this short book. It is, however, one of the main topics of my book: Advanced Reef Keeping II, also published by Aardvark Press. The best advice I can give you is to buy a food developed for the reef aquarium, not some fancy food in a fancy container, that is really meant for fish, and follow the manufacturers instructions, keeping in mind that they are usually conservative. On the other hand, do not over-feed either, as that increases the amount of organic load that your filters will have to deal with, and may, as a result, affect your water quality.

Adding Lifeforms :

Although, technically speaking, not part of husbandry, it is important to be very careful when adding new lifeforms to your tank, especially fish. Make sure that the stock you get is "clean", meaning free of parasites. How is this done ? By placing the fish in a so-called hospital tank for a few days and observing it. Or by treating the fish with medication and using the drip method. Add the fish to your tank only after you have dripped water from the tank into a bucket, where you have placed the fish, and some medicine, for about 45 minutes. Much more on this subject is found in Marine Reef and Advanced Reef Keeping II.

6. Miscellaneous mixed short Topics

Small Reef Aquarium Basics is by no means an encyclopedic work. I tried to cover as much of what I felt was necessary for the average Hobbyist to know, to set up a successful reef aquarium, without incurring huge expenditures. You may want to read up on some of the more basic topics in other books. I have recommended a few, and particularly like Martin Moe's : The Marine Aquarium Reference. There are a few topics, however, that I briefly want to address in these last pages :

Heating and Cooling :

You must try to keep the temperature of the reef tank stable. The one I recommend is between 75 and 77 F°. Whether that requires heaters, in your case, is something only you can decide. If the tank is in a cool, perhaps air-conditioned room, probably yes. Many Hobbyists find that their tanks run too warm. Adding a cooler is of course very expensive. You may have to try and determine why the tank runs so hot. Perhaps the pumps ? Or the lights, especially if no fan extracts the heat from the canope. Usually the problem can be isolated and solved without having to resort to buying a chiller.

Cycling the Tank :

Refer to the many articles that appeared in magazines such as FAMA and Marine Reef, and other books. Doing it the right way is a very important part of ending up with a successful tank, and you should read up on this process before starting your aquarium. The more you know, the better off you, and your tank will be.

Instrumentation :

Although I do not advocate fancy controllers and instruments for the basic reef tank, there are some of you who will want to acquire some form of electronic control method over pH, and perhaps redox potential. That is of course fine. Buy instrumentation that was developed for the reef tank, not something that is offered for sale but was originally made for industry, where "rough" rather than "precise" measurements are the norm. Lab equipment is of course great, but so will the price be. And if you do buy such equipment, the one thing to look for is the degree of accuracy it offers, e.g. in the case of a redox unit, how many millivolt, or what percentage of the scale. For example, a 1% of scale error on a meter that can show from -1999 to +1999 is 40 mv. Take heed. On a meter running from -999 to +999 the error is still 20 mv. Be aware that the reason certain instruments cost more is very simple: they are accurate, or should I say much more accurate. I know of only three companies that make such instruments specifically for the hobby : Sanders, Tunze and Thiel•Aqua•Tech, which has them manufactured in the USA.

Pen-type meters are all right, but be aware that they may not be all that accurate. If you can live with that, then buy as an educated consumer, knowing that the reading you get may be somewhat off. If you decide to get some form of instrument, the one I recommend you get first, is a redox potential meter, and buy a real good electrode, not general purpose types, so often advertised in magazines. You may even want to buy the electrode from someone else, e.g. a company such as Cole Parmer in Chicago, who offer a very wide variety of electrodes, controllers and meters. I personally use the Hach, refillable, liquid double junction electrodes, and have been extremely satisfied with them, but they are expensive, much more, for instance, than a Broadley James.

Instruments, especially controller type instruments, make one's life easier, and tank conditions very stable, but greatly add to the cost of the tank. And that is not what we had in mind when writing this book. If you want to know how to install such automated aquariums, you may want to read my other books.

Equipment such as Reactors :

Several companies offer pressure operated reactors for various purposes, e.g. oxygen, ozone, carbon dioxide, carbonate hardness, and so on. Although they definitely assist in maintaining a more stable environment, I do not consider them to be part of the small reef, rather, they are positioned somewhere between the basic and the automated reef.

If they are of interest to you, check into the products of companies such as Marine Technical Concepts, Route 4 Marine Tech, my own company, and several others that advertise in the magazines. But before you buy, read up on exactly what these units do, or can do for you.

Of particular interest to many Hobbyists who set up reef tanks is the so-called **oxygen reactor**, described at length in both my other books. Air is forced into a cylinder, usually tall, and mixed with water coming from the sump of the trickle filter, or main water return line to the aquarium. Because air contains oxygen (about 21 %) and because the process operates under over pressure -anywhere from 1 to 5 psi is not uncommon- this oxygen is forced into the water, and super oxygenates the aquarium's water. This type of reactor is beneficial only, if all other methods that you already use (filters, skimmers, ozone), do not result in oxygen saturation. If you already have high levels of dissolved oxygen there is no need, and no benefit, to installing such a reactor.

The **ozone reactor** operates on the same principle. Instead of air alone, a mixture of air and ozone are injected into the reactor. This forces the ozone into the water, which results in dissolved and non dissolved organic material being quickly oxidized, since ozone has a very high oxidative power. This, in turn, results in the redox potential of the water in the tank being raised, meaning the tank's water has become purer, and the living environment for the tank's inhabitants better. Ozone reactors are trickier to adjust than oxygen types, but with a few trial and error settings most Hobbyists do not seem to have any problems with them. Noteworthy about these reactors is that they greatly improve the water quality, but that it is better to operate them if you have some way of measuring the redox potential, **and you must have a residual ozone test.** Because they are so efficient, it is most important that you ensure that the water flowing out of an ozone reactor passes through activated carbon first, as this will remove residual ozone.

In a system that is not overloaded, **ozone** is usually not required to maintain a high water quality. It is my experience, however, that most Hobbyists overload their systems, and tax the filtration too much as a result, requiring them to install an ozonizer on the system as well. For a much more detailed look at ozone, refer to my two other books.

Many other devices are used on reef tanks, e.g. carbon dioxide injection, carbonate hardness reactors, tangential flow filters, specialized resins, highly sophisticated dosing pumps, oxygen/peroxide/marble generators, and so on. I do not consider them part of the Small Reef, and have, as a result, not covered them.

Conclusion :

No book can claim to be complete. Reef Systems are so intricate, that special situations always exist. I have attempted to give you my personal way of setting up a small reef, on a budget that is livable, but will still give a tank that you can be proud of.

Once you have a basic set-up, you can always build on what you already have, and add other devices that help in maintaining and/or improving the water quality. You can view this suggestion as a building block approach, and it is. If, however, you follow generally accepted recommendations on tank load, and do not tax your system by adding more and more animals, without regard for the filtration, you will, in my opinion, not need to add any other devices. All you may want to do, is to add some form of instrumentation that will make testing, and monitoring, a less time consuming task.

I hope you have enjoyed this third book of mine, and welcome any suggestions for additions in future editions. Advanced Reef Keeping Made Simple, and The Marine Fish and Invert Reef Aquarium, take a close look at more automated systems, and although you may not want to set up such a system, you may want to read the books anyway, just to learn more about tank technology. I highly recommend that you subscribe to our newsletter **Marine Reef**, as it will keep you up to date on the latest developments in the Reef Hobby.

Advanced Reef Keeping II, the book dealing with the animal life in the aquarium, may or may not be available when you read this, depending on when you bought this one. Check with your dealer, or with us.

Good luck in your endeavors. Call Thiel•Aqua•Tech anytime you have questions that you cannot get resolved. We will try to help you, even if you are not using our equipment. And, please, share your knowledge with other Hobbyists.

Table of Contents